T0332406

Green Internet of Things

Green Internet of Things (IoT) envisions the concept of reducing the energy consumption of IoT devices and making the environment safe. Considering this factor, this book focuses on both the theoretical and implementation aspects in green computing, next-generation networks or smart networks that can be utilized in providing green systems through IoT- enabling technologies, that is, the technology behind its architecture and building components. It also encompasses design concepts and related advanced computing in detail.

- Highlights the elements and communication technologies in Green IoT
- Discusses technologies, architecture and components surrounding Green IoT
- Describes advanced computing technologies in terms of smart world, data centres and other related hardware for Green IoT
- Elaborates energy-efficient Green IoT Design for real-time implementations
- Covers pertinent applications in building smart cities, healthcare devices, efficient energy harvesting and so forth

This short-form book is aimed at students, researchers in IoT, academicians and Industry R&D researchers.

Green Internet of Things

Bandana Mahapatra
Anand Nayyar

CRC Press
Taylor & Francis Group
Boca Raton London

CRC Press is an imprint of the
Taylor & Francis Group, an **informa** business

First edition published 2023
by CRC Press
6000 Broken Sound Parkway NW, Suite 300, Boca Raton, FL 33487–2742

and by CRC Press
4 Park Square, Milton Park, Abingdon, Oxon, OX14 4RN

CRC Press is an imprint of Taylor & Francis Group, LLC

© 2023 Bandana Mahapatra & Anand Nayyar

Library of Congress Cataloging-in-Publication Data
Names: Mahapatra, Bandana, author. | Nayyar, Anand, author.
Title: Green Internet of Things / Bandana Mahapatra, Anand Nayyar.
Description: First edition. | Boca Raton, FL : CRC Press, 2023. |
    Includes bibliographical references and index.
Identifiers: LCCN 2022008907 (print) | LCCN 2022008908 (ebook) |
    ISBN 9781032069135 (hbk) | ISBN 9781032069166 (pbk) |
    ISBN 9781003204503 (ebk)
Subjects: LCSH: Internet of Things. | Electronic apparatus and
    appliances—Energy conservation. | Green electronics.
Classification: LCC TK5105.8857 .M335 2023 (print) | LCC TK5105.8857
    (ebook) | DDC 004.67/8—dc23/eng/20220503
LC record available at https://lccn.loc.gov/2022008907
LC ebook record available at https://lccn.loc.gov/2022008908

ISBN: 978-1-032-06913-5 (hbk)
ISBN: 978-1-032-06916-6 (pbk)
ISBN: 978-1-003-20450-3 (ebk)

DOI: 10.1201/9781003204503

Typeset in Times
by Apex CoVantage, LLC

Contents

Preface

The rapid growth of digital technology has transformed the overall industry in almost every sector. The upward trend seen in the use of smartphones, laptops and the internet along with networking systems undergoing heavy revolution with technological advancements has affected the lifestyle of both urban and rural areas to a huge extent. People enjoy the flexibility of using heterogeneous systems to connect from anywhere and everywhere, which has made the use of smart and flexible devices quite popular and creating a huge demand for the Internet of Things (IoT) concept. IoT is applied over global network infrastructures, including various device elements, for example, sensors, actuators and appliances, which are implanted into various physical objects capable of sensing, processing and communicating information over networks. Billions of devices are connected with a huge volume of data being transferred over networks and processed via a variety of connected processors. In addition, communication and network devices are required to provide uninterrupted connection for the Quality of Service (QoS) of the system. The QoS criteria cause these network elements and devices to consume more energy as well as emit huge quantities of carbon footprints and other harmful gases into the environment, posing a threat of global warming to the ecosystem. This calls for a need to focus on energy-efficient aspects of the components that compose the IoT system along with making them eco-friendly. Thus, the issue of energy consumption in IoT-based systems can strike a balance between offering QoS and environmental safety is an important research focus.

The concept of Green IoT is about "energy-efficient IoT" that works towards energy optimization as well as reducing the greenhouse effect caused by already-existing applications for implementing and scaling IoT in various industrial sectors.

This book comprises five chapters, which provide in-depth, comprehensive information about every aspect of Green IoT. **Chapter 1**, titled *Introduction to the Fundamentals of Internet of Things*, highlights the concept of IoT, its technical background, architecture, models and applications over various domains. **Chapter 2**, *The Elements of Green Internet of Things: Architecture and Components*, discusses in detail the various elements of Green IoT systems, the architectural background as well as device components. **Chapter 3**, *Advanced Computing for Green Internet of Things*, elaborates on various advanced technologies and the integration of green components to achieve a Green

IoT system. **Chapter 4**, *Energy-Efficient Design towards Green Internet of Things*, integrates and elaborates various proposed optimization-based designs proposed by researchers, which support reducing energy consumption as well as integrating green components into various elements of IoT, leading them towards a Green IoT system. **Chapter 5**, *Impact and Application of Green Internet of Things in Various Fields*, highlights the application areas for implementing Green IoT, its benefits and impact on the environment as well as the various techniques that can be adopted to convert an existing IoT system into a "Green IoT System."

We thank all the reviewers for making the book a huge success.

Bandana Mahapatra
Anand Nayyar

Authors

Dr. Bandana Mahapatra received her B.Tech. degree from Krupajal Engineering College, Bhubaneswar, India in 2005; M.Tech. degree from the Institute of Technical Education and Research, BPUT, in 2008; and Ph.D. degree from Siksha 'O' Anusandhan University, in 2018. She is currently working as Assistant Professor with the Symbiosis Skills and Professional University, School of Data Science. She has eight years of expertise in teaching, entrepreneurship and research and development, with a specialization in computer science engineering subjects. She has been granted 10 Indian patents and has published 20+ research papers in reputed SCI/SCOPUS journals from Springer, Elsevier and Bentham Science; and seven articles in reputed Scopus indexed international conferences including IEEE, Springer and Elsevier. She has authored more than 12 chapters in reputed publications such as CRC, SJM, and IGI Global Publications with many more still in the pipeline. Her research interests are security, IoT, artificial intelligence, swarm optimization, cloud security, ad hoc network, and many more.

Dr. Anand Nayyar received his Ph.D. (Computer Science) from Desh Bhagat University in 2017 in the area of wireless sensor networks and swarm intelligence. He is currently working in the School of Computer Science–Duy Tan University, Da Nang, Vietnam as Assistant Professor, Scientist, Vice-Chairman (Research) and Director-IoT and Intelligent Systems Lab. He is a certified professional with 100+ professional certificates from CISCO, Microsoft, Oracle, Google, Beingcert, EXIN, GAQM, Cyberoam and many more. He has published more than 150+ research papers in various high-quality ISI-SCI/SCIE/ SSCI Impact Factor journals cum Scopus/ESCI indexed journals; 100+ papers at international conferences indexed with Springer, IEEE Xplore and ACM Digital Library; 40+ book chapters in various Scopus Web of Science indexed books with Springer, CRC Press, Elsevier and more with citations: 6000+, H-index: 40 and I-Index: 150. He is a member of more than 50+ associations as a senior and life member, including IEEE and ACM. He has authored/co-authored as well as edited 30+ books on computer science. He is associated with more than 500+ international conferences as programme committee/chair/advisory board/review board member. He has 18 Australian patents, 50 Indian design cum utility patents, 3 Indian copyright, 2 Canadian copyrights and 5 German patents to his credit in the areas of wireless communications, artificial intelligence, cloud computing, IoT and image processing. He has been awarded 40+ awards for teaching and research—Young Scientist, Best Scientist, Young Researcher Award, Outstanding Researcher Award, Excellence in Teaching and many more. He is acting as Associate Editor for *Wireless Networks* (Springer), *Computer Communications* (Elsevier), *International Journal of Sensor Networks* (IJSNET) (Inderscience), *Frontiers of Computer Science, PeerJ Computer Science, Human Centric Computing and Information Sciences* (HCIS), *IET-Quantum Communications, IET Wireless Sensor Systems, IET Networks, IJDST, IJISP, IJCINI* and *IJGC*. He is acting Editor-in-Chief at *IGI-Global* for a USA journal titled the *International Journal of Smart Vehicles and Smart Transportation* (IJSVST). He has reviewed more than 2,000+ articles for various Web of Science indexed journals. His current research focuses on the areas of wireless sensor networks, IoT, swarm intelligence, cloud computing, artificial intelligence, drones, blockchain, cyber security, network simulation and wireless communications.

Introduction to the Fundamentals of Internet of Things

1

---

1 INTRODUCTION TO INTERNET OF THINGS

The concept of Internet of Things (IoT) is currently considered one of the significant fields of technological development contributing to the future generation of the digital era. It is well stated that every single entity or object in the future electronic world will be digitally connected over the internet with one another. Even common day-to-day products such as vehicles equipped with software and sensors, various components from technically equipped industries will be efficiently combined with a common network revolutionizing people's day-to-day lifestyles. Visionary scientists have rightly predicted that there will be a vigorous impact of IoT over the fields of digital network platforms and the overall economy where they claim that almost 100 billion electronic devices will be connected with one another causing an impact of increases of about $11 trillion by the year 2025, which is being addressed in various conference reports, news articles and gaining a lot of limelight.

The massive implementation of various IoT devices at a large scale has pledged to bring about a remarkable change to multiple aspects of our lifestyles [1–2].

DOI: 10.1201/9781003204503-1

Currently, many novel IoT-based network-equipped products, e.g., internet-enabled appliances, home automation components and home energy management-based devices are gradually taking us into the world of "smart homes," which are quite effective in terms of security and energy efficiency [2].

Apart from these, various other personal healthcare IoT-based devices, such as wearable fitness and health monitoring devices and network-enabled medical devices, are currently transforming the way healthcare services are delivered [1].

The technology claims to provide support for senior citizens or people suffering from physical impairments, promising improved lifestyles at affordable costs.

A few IoT-based systems like intelligent traffic systems, sensor-equipped roads and smart traffic systems are slowly moving society towards a smart city concept apart from making our world a comfortable place to reside, as well as minimize energy consumption. The concept of IoT offers a transformation of methods that are currently a part of agriculture, industry, energy production and distribution.

Researchers are currently working on the prospective impact of the "IoT revolution", where they have highlighted concerns regarding issues pertaining to security, privacy and technical interoperability [3].

The implementation of IoT in real-life applications has given way to varieties of other challenges that need to be addressed.

Various industries and research organizations have put forth adverse side effects of IoT that may cause a strong negetive impact over the world economy within a span of next 5 to 10 years. A few of the concerns, which have been highlighted by researchers are as follows:

Evolvement of Internet of Things

Though the term "Internet of Things" has been coined recently, the underlying technology had been there since long. The technology works by connecting together various architecturally diverse devices like computer networks to monitor, control devices, etc., which is probably some decades-old concept. Until the late 1970s, electric grids and telephone lines were connected together for creating remote monitoring machines. The sudden evolution of wireless technology gave way to the concept of machine to machine, which is technically termed the "M2M concept." The concept of M2M gave way to multiple solution design for control and monitoring purpose becoming popular in industry. The early M2M proposed solutions were designed based on industry-specific standards instead of Internet Standards, i.e., IP-based Standards [4–5].

The concept of connecting heterogeneous devices over the internet using IP was never a novel concept. The idea came into existence during 1990 in a conference article that featured operating a toaster remotely over the internet connected through IP. Since then multiple electronic devices were tried being remotely operated via IP control examples, a soda machine connected and experimented at Carnegie Mellon University or a coffee pot in Trojan room at University of Cambridge, UK. These minor experiments laid the foundation of a robust field of research and development, which is what today is the buzzword IoT, and has gained an enormous pace of development at a broad prospective with progression of several technology and market trends. This benign initial experimentation made way to connecting more and more devices cheaply as well as easily giving way to the evolution of "Smart Object Networking" [6].

McKinsey Global Institute has explained a wide range of possible applications in their report, "Unlocking the Potential of the Internet of Things," that covers a wide range of potential industrial applications of IoT. Apart from this, multiple established organizations have tried developing various applications and used cases of IoT such as integrated location-based smart cities or smart homes. Considering the wide range of domains evolving based on IoT-based devices, scientists and industry predict that the use of IoT may extend to almost every aspect of our day-to-day lives [6–7].

This assumption in the industry has triggered companies into estimating that the futuristic network/internet traffic generated by non-PC devices may see a leap from 40% to 70% by 2030.

In 2014, Cisco conducted a survey where it forecast the increase in M2M machine usage in domestic, healthcare, automotive and other IoT verticals by 19% [8].

1.1 TECHNOLOGY BEHIND THE INTERNET OF THINGS

The technology behind IoT is complicated, powerful and well organized with the IoT elements where mesh blends together perfectly as shown in Figure 1.1, making a unique IoT architecture with proper device management.

The concept and applications of IoT are not just limited to home and urban automation but also have the power to improve our day-to-day lives as well as the ways we function as a society, which has the potential to reform

FIGURE 1.1   Interconnected Mesh and IoT Elements

the business execution method, ultimately perceiving various aspects of the world [8–9].

1.1.1 Why Do You Need a Robust Internet of Things Architecture?

The reforms that are anticipated by venturing to IoT in our lives are huge; nevertheless, we are all aware of the famous quote: "Rome was not built in a day." The life-changing contribution of IoT can be seen happening in dribs and drabs rather than in giant leaps. The major reason for IoT progress not moving in leaps and bounds is due to the inherent diversity of IoT systems integrating together heterogeneous systems as shown in Figure 1.2, which hinders the growth of IoT systems [10].

Two major challenges blocking the growth of IoT are security and fragmentation. Fragmentation happens to be at the core of IoT due to the diverse nature of devices that are connected into a system. Making any IoT system work needs harnessing various resources, i.e., hardware, software, systems etc. These diverse systems are put together within a single framework to make it well-integrated, reliable and cost-effective [11–12].

The IoT concept needs a strong foundation as the IoT architecture, which can serve the designed purpose. The infrastructure quality solely determines the efficiency and applicability of the system.

FIGURE 1.2   IoT Systems and Architecture

1.2 BUILDING BLOCKS UNDERLYING INTERNET OF THINGS ARCHITECTURE

While every IoT system is different, the foundation for each IoT architecture as well as its general data process flow is roughly the same. First, it consists of the things, which are objects connected to the internet that by means of their embedded sensors and actuators are able to sense the environment around them and gather information which is then passed on to IoT gateways [13]. The next stage consists of IoT data acquisition systems and gateways that collect the great mass of unprocessed data, convert it into digital streams and filter and pre-process it so that it is ready for analysis. The third layer is represented by edge devices responsible for further processing and enhanced analysis of data. This layer is also where visualization and machine learning technologies may step in. After that, the data is transferred to data centres, which can be either cloud based or installed locally. This is where the data is stored, managed and analysed in depth for actionable insights.

The IoT architecture can be segregated into four groups as shown in Figure 1.3.

    a. IoT Devices
    b. Sensors/Actuators
    c. Analytics and Data Processing
    d. Controllers

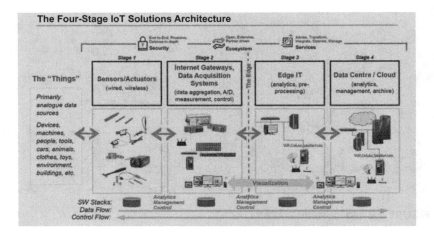

FIGURE 1.3   The Four Stages of IoT Architecture

In almost any IoT system, the wide variety of connected devices are solely responsible for providing quality data, which may be considered as the core of IoT systems. In order to catch the physical parameters from the real-world environment or the object itself, i.e., data, the system needs to be equipped with strong sensors or actuators. The actuators or sensors are embedded within the device or implemented in the form of stand-alone objects capable of capturing and measuring real-time data, for example, agricultural sensors designed for measuring parameters like air, soil, temperature and humidity, soil pH levels or crop exposure to sunlight [13–14].

Sensors and Actuators

The actuators work hand-in-hand with the sensors to convert the real-time data generated by the sensors using equipment such as smart objects. For example, a smart watering system-equipped necessary sensors and actuators where input provided by the sensors analyses the situation before generating the command to open selected water valves located in places where soil humidity is found below the predefined threshold. These valves remain open until the sensors collect the data and provide a report of values being restored to default [15].

The entire method of systems operation is automated without human intervention, keeping in mind that the system connection should not only connect objects that can communicate in bi-direction with respective gateways or data acquisition systems but also gather information from each other and share

FIGURE 1.4   IoT Architecture for M2M Devices

information and collaborate with each other in real time in order to leverage the benefit of the system as a whole.

Achieving complete automation, communicating and sharing information among the connected devices is not an easy task, specifically in battery-operated devices that since such communication consumes a huge amount of power, energy as well as bandwidth. Only a robust IoT architecture as described in Figure 1.4 can support efficient device management subject to its supporting secure and lightweight communication protocol like lightweight M2M. Lightweight M2M can be considered the leading standard protocol found to be suitable for managing low-power lightweight devices, which is quite popular and in use by many IoT cases [12, 14].

Gateways and Data Acquisition

The gateways and data acquisition layers work in close proximity with sensors and networks and play a significant role in IoT architecture as shown in Figure 1.5. They are responsible for data collection, filtering and transferring the data to edge infrastructure and cloud-based platforms.

Considering the huge volumes of real-time data captured by sensors and actuators as input and output results in the deployment of millions of devices, the

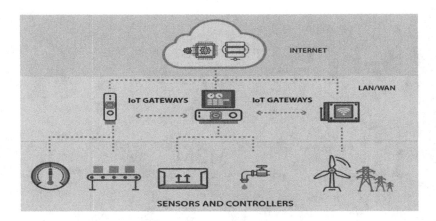

FIGURE 1.5 Gateway Sensors and Controllers in IoT Architecture

primary focus of which is to aggregate, select and transfer the given data. They serve as the connecting points clubbing up the remaining layers together.

Gateways support communication among the sensors and the underlying system by converting the sensor data captured into formats that are easily compatible, transferable as well as usable for divergent system components [15].

Gateways also provide a local pre-processing of the data, filter the data and minimize the volume of information required to be transmitted to the cloud, which can possibly reduce response time as well as the transmission cost. The pre-processed data is thereafter squeezed into useful bundles that are ready for further processing.

Security may be considered one of the major challenges while implementing the functionalities of gateways, considering the fact that they are responsible for bidirectional management of data flow. The gateway software with support of proper encryption and security tools can prevent security-related challenges like cloud data leaks, risk of malicious outside attacks on IoT devices etc.

Edge Analytics

Edge devices are not considered an indispensable component in an IoT architecture, but use of edge devices can bring about major differences in terms of benefits, typically in large-scale IoT projects. Edge systems provide quick response times and offer flexibility in the processing and analysis of IoT data irrespective of the limited accessibility as well as the speed of transmission of IoT cloud platforms.

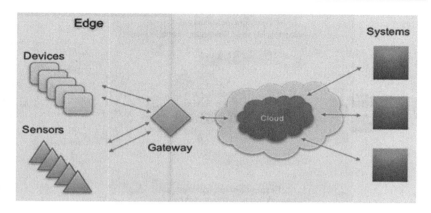

FIGURE 1.6   Cloud and Gateways in IoT Architecture

Since for many industrial applications based on the IoT concept, use of edge computing systems is undergoing a rapid growth in popularity among other industrial IoT ecosystems [15–16].

The edge infrastructure is physically located near the data source. This close proximity enables the device to act upon the IoT material fast in real-time, providing an output in form of instant actionable intelligence.

Such systems are considered beneficial when large chunks of data are required to be processed and are dependent on the power of the cloud for its processing, as described in Figure 1.6. Reducing the exposure to long network for data routing offers lots of benefits such as enhanced security aspects with reduction in the power as well as the bandwidth consumption, which contributes positively towards being an effective business resource [17].

Data Centre/Cloud Platform

Describing sensors as neurons and gateways is the backbone of IoT, and the cloud may be defined as the brain in the IoT body as described in Figure 1.7. Quite contrary to edge solutions, the data centres play a major role in storing, processing as well as analysing huge quantities of data. Here the goal of the system is to extract deeper insights from the data using powerful data analytics tool, engines and machine learning mechanisms that are well equipped in the data centres unlike those in edge computing systems. Hence, edge computing systems fail in supporting a deep dive into the data. In the past several years, cloud computing significantly contributed towards incurring high production rates, reducing unplanned downtime and energy consumption in addition to providing several other benefits [16–17].

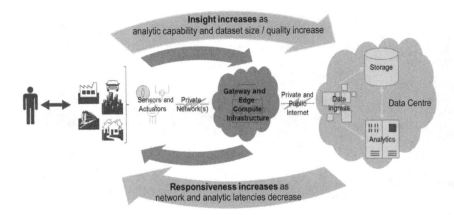

FIGURE 1.7   Edge Compute Infrastructure for Data Centres/Cloud Platform IoT

Provided appropriate user application solutions are furnished to the cloud, it can provide options like business intelligence and presentation, which supports human system interaction towards making informed decisions on the basis of reports, dashboards and data that can be viewed in real time.

1.3 INTERNET OF THINGS COMMUNICATION MODELS

The IoT systems operation can be categorized roughly into four technical communication models with respect to their operational format and mode. In 2015, the Internet Architecture Board (IAB) issued a document covering the guidelines for networking of smart objects (RFC 7452), which roughly covers the framework of four common communication models that can be adopted by IoT devices. With the new pandemic phase cropping up, the communication models may see a shift into including techniques that can provide solutions to a few of the problems generated by COVID-19, offering an improvisation over existing models [18].

The communication model frameworks and their key features to be considered are discussed as follows.

1.3.1 Connectivity-Based Models

Various recent trends have caught momentum aggravating the growth of IoT and its prominence during 2021 from various data-intensive experiences, which use various IoT devices, e.g., self-driving cars or health- and safety-related IoT-based systems. All throughout, the concept of the IoT landscape remains in fragments with multiple prevailing standards and connectivity options, which are all the more versatile in nature rather than following a standard form leading to what is referred to as "connectivity chaos." Technically, the connectivity needed by a smart vehicle is different from a wearable device or a piece of machinery on a factory floor. Although 5G is currently considered as the most desirable communication standard, the industry needs to focus on other connectivity/network-based communication models suitable to their data for transmission. "The connectivity has to be considered based on the use case," as quoted by Pelino. Moreover, focus on 5G connectivity fails to factor the growth of satellite and other low-power networking technologies, which as predicted will see an increase by 20%. [19].

1.3.2 Communication Models for Smart Building Technology

Smart building technology is expected to support and trigger employee transformation, which tends to concentrate less over the old preferential data such as energy-efficiency, worker productivity etc. In lieu, during 2021 post-pandemic, the scenario will see a shift where smart building technology will centre more on core priorities, such as worker health and safety. For example, in the past, smart building technologies were typically used to assign conference rooms for meetings and use IoT-based smart lights and thermometers for energy efficiency, which may shift now to worker social distancing and track-and-trace capabilities in order to minimize COVID-19 spread [18–19].

1.3.3 Connected Machines

Multiple manufacturing plants as well as other environments equipped with expensive machines in this phase of pandemic taken to remote monitoring. "Having remote monitoring capabilities is currently quite prevalent in pandemic scenario," well quoted by Pelino, where the ones who had never activated remote monitoring in past are currently moving towards these IoT based features of the machine. He further highlighted that "remote monitoring has undergone a trial by fire in the post-pandemic era, and many organizations have now embraced these capabilities to the extent that they are not going to part them off even in post pandemic scenario."

In contradiction, in 2020, *IoT World Today* conducted an IoT adoption survey, which was also coherent with the previously stated prediction where 57% of the sample population responded with artificial intelligence and machine learning, taking over performance monitoring aspects, with remote monitoring IoT technologies in manufacturing facing a slower than expected adoption curve [1].

1.3.4 Consumer and Employee Location Data-Based Communication Models

Currently, with the advent of recent trends in e-commerce, various retail stores have explored curbside pickup and other location-based services in order to reach out to customers during the pandemic. The background idea was using the location-based data for enhancing customer services, e.g., use of global positioning systems (GPS) in phones to locate customer orders automatically. In addition, quite a number of upcoming features can be added due to the development of IoT, such as check-in at a location via phone to maintain social distance, avoiding physical waiting in lines.

1.4 IOT APPLICATIONS

IoT technology has currently found its way into multiple domains, making itself applicable across various industries. A few of IoT use cases are discussed as follows.

1.4.1 Agriculture and Pest Control

Agriculture industry is one of the essential domains that fulfils the basic needs of all human beings. Currently, in the majority of developed and developing countries where technology is soaring, agro industry is one of the most overlooked or neglected areas to be considered for research and development. However, the way the population across the world is multiplying, very soon it will be challenging to meet the demands of the human population without large-scale agriculture undergoing some major revolution.

Clubbing IoT applications with farming can boost the production rate to maintain the same level as population growth.

IoT-based applications for agro industry can bring about precision in farming by using analytical data for better understanding of soil, moisture level, climatic changes, plant requirement, and so on, as well as boost the yield of agricultural products and encourage efficient use of resources.

IoT-enabled smart devices can also be used for livestock management, which aims at eradicating the problem of pest infiltration by use of sensors to track pest population [18–19].

1.4.2 Environment

Human activities have in many ways, directly or indirectly, harmed our environment to a huge extent. Once realized, technology has moved a step towards tackling various environmental issues. One of these issues is preservation of honeybees. In the current scenario, honeybees are facing threats due to the pollution caused in the atmosphere that has increased the temperature humidity making the environment non-congenial for the bees to grow.

With the help of IoT devices, the beekeeper can take good care of preserving the hives. Using well-connected IoT and sensors, beekeepers can keep track of hive temperature, quantity of food available in the hives and the amount of pollen collected, helping to preserve the environment all the more [20].

1.4.3 Smart Home Applications

One of the most promising areas of IoT applications is smart homes, which are considerably the most common of all other uses of IoT. The smart home concept has practically been built upon the internet as a major component.

The concept of smart home operates on the active use of IoT, where smart home devices collect as well as share information with each other over an integrated platform. The entire series of actions is automated based on the owner's choice of events.

A smart home works with the active use of IoT applications. Smart home devices collect and share information with one another on an integrated platform and automate their actions based on the owner's preference, for example, smart lighting, temperature regulation, thermostats etc. [18–20].

1.4.4 Health Care

IoT has redefined the entire healthcare sector, including physicians, patients, hospitals and health insurance companies. IoT-based healthcare devices like fitness bands and real-time blood pressure devices have become common household requirements for people suffering from such types of health ailments. IoT-based devices are also equipped with alert mechanisms to notify doctors or other family members during emergencies. It assists doctors as well as physicians to collect case histories of patients via IoT devices and access real-time health data easily.

Availability of real-time data can be quite helpful during clinical trials. IoT devices can also assist hospitals by tracking location of various medical devices, defibrillators or wheelchairs, even for the purpose of inventory management, environmental monitoring, temperature regulation etc.

The data collected by IoT devices is generally stored in the cloud, which are easily accessible by medical insurance companies that can track the regular health records of patients, taking note of their lifestyle and activities [21,23].

1.4.5 Smart Cities

Many developed countries are undergoing the idea of planning smart cities, where IoT can be considered one of the building blocks of this architecture based on several planned activities such as efficient traffic management, public transportation, smart sensor-based parking, automated utility billing, which can be practically implemented improving the overall quality of life [23–24].

The combination of sensors, GPS data collection and cloud platforms will make it easier to monitor traffic conditions over a given geographic area, by suggesting alternative routes when and where required, with planned construction programs, which can predict upcoming traffic. Smart billing systems for homes with efficient use of energy, smart street lighting, can increase public safety with the use of smart surveillance cameras or smart microphones for assisting in crime and accident detection in any area across a city are few classic examples where IoT plays a major role in implementation of the smart city concept across the globe.

Smart cities can be expressed as a large-scale IoT-based application world, which in reality defines the implemented future digital era in our day-to-day lives [25].

1.4.6 Safe Driving

The extensive use of mobile phones while driving has drastically increased the rate of road accidents. The amount of warnings against the use of mobile phones while driving has changed the attitude of callous drivers or the youth. Nevertheless, with the help of IoT technology, currently it is possible to track drivers using phones while driving and block the distractive apps from their phones while in motion. IoT has also found its place in trying to analyse driver behaviour and identify drivers that need to undergo coaching based upon their driving patterns.

The recent development of driverless cars has brought about a new revolution in the automotive sector. These cars are designed on strong IoT connected with multiple advanced sensors and gyroscopes interacting together to carry forward a self-driven autonomous car.

Here, a huge quantity of data is collected over real time and transmitted using a common platform, which is expected to guide the cars regarding traffic conditions, potholes, sharp-turn speed breakers etc. [22].

1.4.7 Waste Management

Considering the current environmental conditions, it is important to take measures to the preserve atmosphere and air quality around us. The cleanliness and sanitation of human beings are currently big concerns that have attracted attention as one of the results of the outbreak of the coronavirus that targets our lower immunity conditions. The degradable waste generated by humans, in terms of dry and wet waste, needs to be effectively disposed of in order to maintain our health.

IoT has tried to solve this issue using IoT-based applications that can notify disposal truck drivers about filled dustbins informing them about the route, which will help in locating the trash rather than wasting time trying to locate them while exploring locations with empty bins.

IoT devices may assist in developing smart bins that can auto-segregate trash categories like plastic, metal, glass or paper from wet waste such as remnant food items and other eatables.

1.4.8 Tackling Industrial Issues

It is not wrong to say that the Industrial Revolution is not possible without practical implementation of IoT. IoT has quite a significant number of used cases with respect to automating the industrial sector, which is the next-generation industrialization, "Industry 4.0." IoT can assist in both asset management and inventory management, where integrating IoT with the manufacturing sector assists in tracking the effectiveness of the systems being used, identification of errors if any in the machinery or any accidental occurrences of unplanned downtime [25].

1.4.9 Supply Chain

IoT can assist the supply chain process by providing a tracking of the goods in the transit phase, collecting customer feedback automatically and improvising and optimizing the supply chain workflow. It also helps both suppliers and drivers to better preserve goods and items under transit via conveying statistics about temperature, pressure and other environmental conditions.

1.5 INTERNET OF THINGS ARCHITECTURE: A CASE STUDY

The healthcare sector is one of the prominent industries that have accepted and adopted IoT concept to the fullest, therefore has applied used cases to the maximum. The functionality and the quality of improvisation and care for patients that can be brought about by integrating IoT are enormous, which is reason enough to incorporate IoT systems and devices wherever applicable [23].

The healthcare sector includes few key applications such as patient enhancement in terms of personal safety and security, optimal cost incurred in healthcare by cost cutting unnecessary items and providing appropriate support at required times via usage of IoT-based smart medical devices or emergency systems.

Considering the huge population and its imposed challenges, one of the major concerns in the healthcare domain are ailments related to old age, e.g., diabetes and heart disease. Here, prevention acts quite vitally when the aim is to provide better health for elderly patients. This requirement makes IoT one of the sought-after technologies with reliability, security and real-time precise control at prime focus.

One IoT-based industry has identified the desirability of an architecture for an automatic monitoring system for senior citizens that will collect data and perform a real-time analysis and provide network connectivity for accessing various infrastructure-level services and an application that can support both user interface and display. The designed architecture needs to include body sensors that can collect patient data and gateways that can filter as well as forward collected data, and analysis and wireless transmission of data to the cloud can be done by microcontrollers and microprocessors. Moreover, the communication tool has also been integrated that can transfer data to various remote locations, e.g., emergency services and healthcare providers with the intention of monitoring and tracking [23,24].

The IoT architectural design for the healthcare system proposed should be a three-layered architecture consisting of:

1. Physical stage,
2. Communication stage and
3. Application stage.

The first layer design, i.e., the physical layer, is integrated with a multiple sensor network, which can evaluate patients' vital records and readings such as nutrition, medical intake, physical activities etc. This layer is also equipped with a monitoring network that consists of in-house sensors and actuators, which are responsible for maintaining air quality, temperature and analysing as well as determining beforehand the probable occurrence of any serious symptoms for the patient.

The second layer of the design architecture consists majorly of IoT devices that can collect various pieces of information received by the sensors, convert them into meaningful data streams and finally forward them to a back-end destination.

The third layer includes cloud-based analytical engines with imbibed machine learning mechanisms. In this layer, data is received, stored and processed using cloud-based data analysis engines and machine learning mechanisms. The insights and information extracted from this data are typically used to improvise treatment, enhance the connected device mechanisms and enable proper healthcare services for all possible scenarios or used for future research and management purposes.

The designed healthcare monitoring system must give access to two different users, which may include healthcare providers, the patient and any family member or caregiver. One of the major concerns of using an IoT-based healthcare system is implementing data security and privacy in such heterogeneous systems. The security in these environments can be implemented by enabling techniques such as encryption of the data being transferred or using a microprocessor that ensures and provides a secured encryption and communication method through SSL (Secured socket Layer).

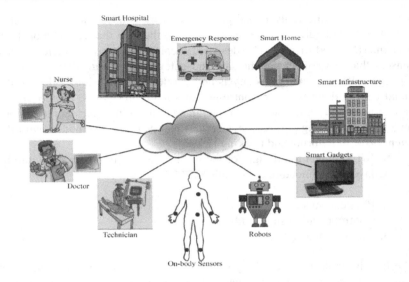

FIGURE 1.8   IoT for Healthcare System

1.6 CONCLUSION

IoT can be considered a game-changing technology that is affecting multiple industries. Many companies and industries are opting for IoT-based systems and applications dragging the traditional industry more into the smart concept of Industry 4.0. With time, multiple companies and civic bodies are adopting IoT-based applications, slowly transforming into a smart world with smart solutions. IoT has given both businesses and governments many options to improve their work and become more efficient with time and technology.

REFERENCES

[1] D. Giusto, A. Iera, G. Morabito, L. Atzori (Eds.), *The Internet of Things*, Springer, 2010. ISBN: 978-1-4419-1673-0.
[2] National Intelligence Council, "Disruptive Civil Technologies—Six Technologies with Potential Impacts on US Interests out to 2025," *Conference Report CR 2008–07*, April 2008, http://www.dni.gov/nic/NIC_home.html.

[3] INFSO D.4 Networked Enterprise & RFID INFSO G.2 Micro & Nanosystems, "Co-operation with the Working Group RFID of the ETP EPOSS," *Internet of Things in 2020, Roadmap for the Future, Version 1.1*, 27 May 2008.

[4] Auto-Id Labs. http://www.autoidlabs.org/.

[5] The EPCglobal Architecture Framework, EPCglobal Final Version 1.3, Approved 19 March 2009. www.epcglobalinc.org.

[6] K. Sakamura, "Challenges in the Age of Ubiquitous Computing: A Case Study of T-Engine—An Open Development Platform for Embedded Systems," *Proceedings of ICSE'06*, Shanghai, China, May 2006.

[7] M. Presser, A. Gluhak, "The Internet of Things: Connecting the Real World with the Digital World, EURESCOM mess@ge," *Magazine for Telecom Insiders*, vol. 2, 2009, http://www.eurescom.eu/message.

[8] M. Botterman, "For the European Commission Information Society and Media Directorate General, Networked Enterprise & RFID Unit—D4," *Internet of Things: An Early Reality of the Future Internet, Report of the Internet of Things Workshop*, Prague, Czech Republic, May 2009.

[9] B. Sterling, *Shaping Things—Mediawork Pamphlets*, MIT Press, 2005.

[10] ITU Internet Reports, The Internet of Things, November 2005.

[11] A. Dunkels, J.P. Vasseur, "IP for Smart Objects, Internet Protocol for Smart Objects (IPSO) Alliance," *White Paper #1*, September 2008. http://www.ipso-alliance.org.

[12] J. Hui, D. Culler, S. Chakrabarti, "6LoWPAN: Incorporating IEEE 802.15.4 into the IP Architecture—Internet Protocol for Smart Objects (IPSO) Alliance," *White Paper #3*, January 2009.

[13] N. Gershenfeld, R. Krikorian, D. Cohen, The Internet of Things, *Scientific American*, vol. 291, no. 4, pp. 76–81, 2004.

[14] I. Toma, E. Simperl, G. Hench, "A Joint Roadmap for Semantic Technologies and the Internet of Things," *Proceedings of the Third STI Roadmapping Workshop*, Crete, Greece, June 2009.

[15] A. Katasonov, O. Kaykova, O. Khriyenko, S. Nikitin, V. Terziyan, "Smart Semantic Middleware for the Internet of Things," *Proceedings of the Fifth International Conference on Informatics in Control, Automation and Robotics*, Funchal, Madeira, Portugal, May 2008.

[16] W. Wahlster, "Web 3.0: Semantic Technologies for the Internet of Services and of Things," *Lecture at the 2008 Dresden Future Forum*, June 2008, https://www.inderscienceonline.com/doi/pdf/10.1504/IJITCA.2018.090162.

[17] I. Vázquez, "Social Devices: Semantic Technology for the Internet of Things," *Week@ESI*, Zamudio, Spain, June 2009.

[18] https://www.oracle.com/in/internet-of-things/what-is-iot/. (Retrieved on 30 April 2021.)

[19] M. Rouse, "Internet of things (IoT)," *IOT Agenda*, 2019. (Retrieved on 30 April 2021.)

[20] E. Brown, "21 Open Source Projects for IoT," *Linux.com*, September 2016. (Retrieved on 30 April 2021.)

[21] "Internet of Things Global Standards Initiative," *ITU*. (Retrieved on 30 April 2021.)

[22] D. Hendricks, *The Trouble with the Internet of Things*, London Datastore, Greater London Authority. (Retrieved on 30 April 2021.)

[23] Phillip A. Laplante, M. Kassab, Nancy L. Laplante, Jeffrey M. Voas, "Building Caring Healthcare Systems in the Internet of Things," *IEEE Systems Journal*, vol. 12, no. 3: pp. 3030–3037, 2018.

[24] *The "Only" Coke Machine on the Internet*, Carnegie Mellon University. (Retrieved 30 April 2018.)

[25] "Internet of Things Done Wrong Stifles Innovation," *InformationWeek*, 7 July 2014. (Retrieved 30 April 2018.)

The Elements of Green Internet of Things

2

Architecture and Components

2.1 INTRODUCTION

As we know, the Internet of Things (IoT) is currently considered as a worldwide unseen, enticing communication network built on a computing environment that consists of cameras, smart sensors, databases, software and data centres [1]. The Green IoT concept focuses more on using reduced IoT energy and lowering the emissions of CO_2 into the environment.

The concept of Green IoT is mainly about designing, developing and leveraging aspects within an IoT system such as computing devices, communication protocols, energy efficiency, networking architectures to lower CO_2 emissions that may result in reduced pollution while enhancing energy efficiency as shown in Figure 2.1.

The electronic components of machine-to-machine (M2M) architecture for IoT consist of sensors and communication add-ons, where communication devices facilitate the communication process within participating devices while simultaneously sensing the world.

Green IoT mainly consists of three major concepts:

1. Design technologies,
2. Leverage technologies and
3. Enabling technologies.

DOI: 10.1201/9781003204503-2   21

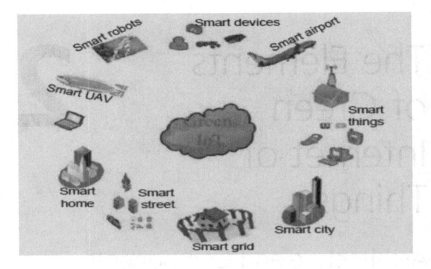

FIGURE 2.1   Components of Green IoT

Design technologies: The concept of design technology is more about involving energy-efficient electronic devices using structured and well-planned communication protocols, network architectures and interconnections.

Leverage technologies: The concept of leverage technology refers to cutting down the rate of carbon emissions and improving energy efficiency. The advent of green ICT technologies has made the green IoT concept quite promising with respect to a few aspects like usage of reduced energy, low hazardous emissions into the atmosphere, less resource consumption and pollution. In due course the concept of Green IoT has made headway in preserving natural resources contributing to taking a baby step against global warming, assuring minimal impact of technology on the environment and human health and lowering the implementation cost significantly.

Hence, it could be rightfully claimed that Green IoT is indeed focusing more on incorporating concepts like green manufacturing, green utilization, green design and green disposal into the traditional process of industry operations [2].

1. *Green use:* The concept of green utilization deals with reducing the power consumption of computers and various other information systems. It includes various energy optimization strategies incorporated within participating electronic devices in order to reduce overall energy consumption, making smart systems that can switch itself

into sleep mode as and when required, devising intelligent load-shedding techniques, for example, a Home Energy Management System, which uses a smart load-balancing scheme that can efficiently distribute the energy supply between current active devices on the home front.

2. *Green disposal:* Green disposal is all about refurbishing and reusing or recycling old systems and unwanted computers or other electronic equipment. The concept is currently being highly adopted for smartphones and laptops where these devices are being sold in second-hand markets at cost-effective prices. One of the leading examples of this concept is in second-hand markets of China.

3. *Green design:* Green design is about developing energy-efficient designs meant for Green IoT, sound components, computers, server cooling equipment etc. Green designs aim at scheming energy-efficient IoT applicable in various domains in order use minimum possible energy as well as taking care of the environment by using biodegradable materials to make green electronic devices that emit a low amount of harmful gases. A few examples for the same are green cloud computing, green data centres, green edge computing etc.

4. *Green manufacturing:* The concept of green manufacturing goes hand in hand with green design, and aims at producing and devising electronic component, computers or various other associated subsystems that have minimal or no impact on the environment.

The chapter aims at providing a detailed description and analysis of the various devices and elements of the Green IoT with respect to its architectural design as well as implementation.

2.2 DESIGN COMPONENTS OF IOT

The various design components which can be adopted for IoT design to improve its usage and efficiency are discussed as follows.

2.2.1 Identification

The process of identification is quite crucial for IoT. The initial discussions in Alliance for Internet of Things Innovation (AIOTI) focused more on the use of communication identifiers like IP addresses and mobile phone numbers in

IoT. These discussions were mostly influenced by the Body of European Regulators for Electronic Communications (BEREC) [1]. However, identification as a component of IoT has a much wider scope of being used with many applications and entities in IoT. Besides identification for communication, it is also applicable in identification of the electronic devices involved and other relevant fields like services, users, data, locations etc. Various existing identification schemes have been standardized and are currently being deployed in the market. Among various system requirements, the identification process plays a major role in providing identification.

The identifiers work like the patterns that are used for uniquely identifying occurrences of single or multiple entity (instance identifier) collection (i.e., type identifier) with respect to a specific context. Various identifier types can be deployed on the basis of the application considered as well as user requirements.

As the IoT concept is all about interaction among heterogeneous devices or things and users by electronic means, both the electronic device and the user have to be identified in order to establish a communication channel among them. The identifier works by providing the identity to an entity.

2.2.2 Sensor-Based Devices

The technology background of IoT innovation has made it possible that we can connect almost every electronic device of our day-to-day lives over the internet. Almost every entity in households, office buildings and factories, including cities, are connected over the network where data and information are collected and used for various purposes, sufficing the quote: "Data is the new oil."

Sensors and other electronic devices are quite important in creating solutions with regard to the IoT concept. These sensors also detect various external pieces of information, replacing it with signals that are clearly identifiable via humans as machines.

Sensors have found applications in various domains or fields like medical, nursing, industry, logistics, transportation, etc., where they play the role of collecting real-time data, irrespective of various conditions and situations, and thus have been found suitable for being deployed in a number of challenging fields, e.g., logistics, transportation, agriculture, disaster prevention, tourism, regional businesses and many more.

With the increased demand in sensors to sense and measure physical phenomena like heat and pressure and human senses such as sight, hearing, touch, taste and smell, sensors can be found almost everywhere. The IoT or Industrial Internet of Things (IIoT) has contributed to bringing the deployment of sensors to a new level.

Sensors are devices that are capable of sensing every change in the environment. The sensors receive input data from various sources such as light, temperature, motion, pressure, etc., providing output of the information if connected to the network with various connected devices or management systems.

Sensors are quite crucial while operating in current domains where they can provide warning signals in the event of major hazards or informing potential issues in business before being blown up, allowing the business to perform predictive maintenance avoiding expensive downtime. The sensor-based data can also undergo analysis for trends providing business owners to gain insight to crucial trends and support them in making informed evidence-based decisions.

The various kinds of sensors designed range in multiple shapes, sizes, etc., which facilitate monitoring as well as measuring multiple data sources, e.g., the brownfield environment that includes various legacy sensors capable of reading digital and analogue input.

A Few Popular Designed IoT-Based Sensor Devices are:

a. *Temperature sensors:* Temperature sensors as shown in Figure 2.2A are electronic sensor devices that are sensitive to heat measurement. They measure the amount of heat energy in a source and detect as well as record temperature changes, converting them into data. The machines that are used for manufacturing need a stable and specific environment with respect to device temperature. Within agriculture, soil temperature may be considered as a key factor for crop growth.

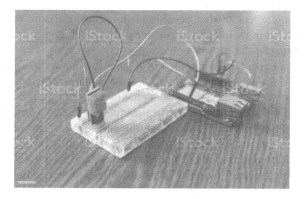

FIGURE 2.2A   Temperature Sensors
Source: https://www.istockphoto.com/photo/humidity-and-temperature-sensor-prototype-at-school-for-iot-device-gm682305606-125286431

FIGURE 2.2B   Humidity Sensors
Source: https://www.electronicshub.org/raspberry-pi-dht11-humidity-temperature-sensor-interface/

b. *Humidity sensors:* Humidity sensor as shown in Figure 2.2B devices measure the presence of water vapour in the atmosphere of the air or presence of any other gases. These sensors are typically found in heating, vents and ACs used in both industry and residential front. They may also be found in many other areas including hospitals and meteorology stations that predict as well as report weather conditions.

c. *Pressure sensors:* A pressure-sensing device as shown in Figure 2.2C senses variations in pressure related to gases and liquids. With the change in pressure, the sensor detects the changes and communicates the same to connected systems. One of the prominent application areas is leak testing, resulting from decay. Pressure sensors are also useful in manufacturing water systems, which needs detection of fluctuations or drops in pressure.

d. *Proximity sensors:* Proximity sensor devices as shown in Figure 2.2D are used for detecting the presence of objects near the sensor. These kinds of sensors radiate electromagnetic fields or infrared rays. Two of the cases used are detection of the motion between a customer and a product and informing users regarding discounts or special offers of products that are located near the sensor. Proximity sensors are also used in the parking lots of malls, stadiums and airports in order to indicate parking availability. They are also used in assembly lines of industry based on chemical, food and other types of industries.

e. *Water Level sensors:* Water level sensor devices as shown in Figure 2.2E can detect the level of the substances including liquids, powders or other granular materials. These sensors are used in many industries

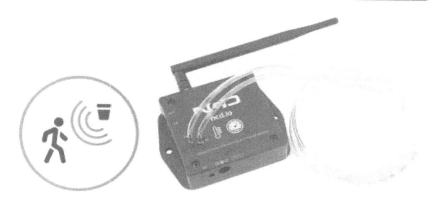

FIGURE 2.2C   Sensor Device to Measure Bidirectional Differential Pressure
Source: https://store.ncd.io/product/iot-long-range-wireless-pressure-sensor-bidirectional-differential/

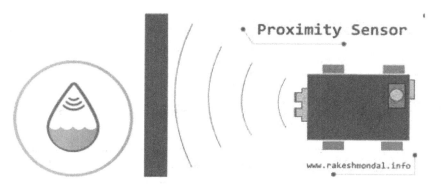

FIGURE 2.2(D)   Proximity Sensors
Source: http://www.infiniteinformationtechnology.com/iot-devices-proximity-sensors

like manufacturing oil or providing water treatment, food or beverage manufacturing etc. Typically, a waste management system provides a commonly used case of water level sensors, which can play a role in detecting of the level of waste in a garbage can or dumpster.

   f. *Accelerometer sensors:* Accelerometer sensors as shown in Figure 2.2F are designed to detect an object's acceleration, i.e., the rate of change of its velocity with respect to time. These sensors can also identify changes to gravity. The application of these devices includes smart pedometers and monitoring driving fleets. These devices can also be used for anti-theft protection that can trigger the system alert, if an object that should be stationary is in motion.

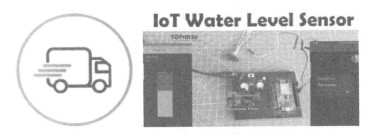

FIGURE 2.2(E)   Water Level Sensors
Source: http://www.infiniteinformationtechnology.com/iot-devices-proximity-sensors

FIGURE 2.2(F)   Accelerometer Sensors
Source: https://www.researchgate.net/figure/Accelerometer-Sensor_fig5_278409659

g. *Gyroscope sensors:* Gryroscope sensors as shown in Figure 2.2G are used for measuring angular rate or velocity, which is often termed as a measurement device for speed and rotation around an axis. Their usage includes automotive industry products, such as car navigation and electronic stability control (anti-skid) systems. Some popular used cases also include motion sensors for video games and camera-shake detection systems.

h. *Gas sensors:* Gas sensors as shown in Figure 2.2H are used to identify changes in air quality including the presence of any toxic, combustible or hazardous gases. The various industries that use gas sensors include mining, oil and gas, chemical research and manufacturing etc. One of the most popular uses is for domestic purposes, i.e., carbon dioxide detectors in homes.

i. *Infrared sensors:* Infrared sensors as shown in Figure 2.2I are devices used for sensing the presence of infrared radiation. These devices can additionally measure heat emitted by objects. Infrared detecting sensors are used in various IoT projects, which include

FIGURE 2.2(G) Gyroscope Sensors
Source: https://www.aliexpress.com/item/32712557239.html

FIGURE 2.2(H) Gas Sensors and Modulators
Source: https://components101.com/articles/introduction-to-gas-sensors-types-working-and-applications

FIGURE 2.2(I) Infrared Sensors
Source: https://robu.in/ir-sensor-working/

FIGURE 2.2(J)   Optical Sensors
Source: https://www.coleparmer.in/p/monarch-instrument-optical-sensors/5681

health care where they contribute to simplifying the monitoring of blood flow and blood pressure. Televisions use infrared sensors to interpret signals sent from a remote control.

Another use of this device is by art historians who use infrared sensors to see hidden layers within paintings in order to help identify an art piece as original or fake or if it has been altered by a restoration process.

j. *Optical sensors:* Optical sensors as shown in Figure 2.2J convert rays of light into electrical signals. There are many applications and uses for optical sensors. In the auto industry, vehicles use optical sensors to recognize signs, obstacles and other things that a driver would notice when driving or parking. Optical sensors play a big role in the development of driverless cars. Optical sensors are very common in smartphones. For example, ambient light sensors can extend battery life. Optical sensors are also used in the biomedical field including breath analysis and heart rate monitors.

MYTHINGS IoT Sensor

The MYTHINGS Smart Sensor as shown in Figure 2.3 defined as a self-contained, battery-powered, multi-purpose IoT sensor that allows capture of critical data points such as acceleration, temperature, humidity, pressure and global positioning system (GPS).

2.2.3 Communication Technologies

The devices participating in IoT systems can communicate in multiple ways via various designed protocols based on their mode of communication. These devices generally consider factors like their geographic locations, their architectural capabilities and the different devices they communicate with. These devices choose protocols designed based on their requirements, i.e., their specific needs.

These IoT designed systems also have considerable constraints to deal with such as power budget, cost limitations, security, geographical regions etc.

In the next section, we discuss the various embedded components of an IoT communication system, their requirements and contexts, which help to identify the best solution for each use case.

2.2.3.1 Components for Internet of Things Device Communication

Generally, IoT systems consist of different architectural components; a few are discussed as follows:

1. *IoT devices:* These are the electronic devices that play a major role in collecting real-time data, be it temperature sensors or giant industrial robots. They are responsible for data collection via sensing the given environments and communicating the same to other devices connected to the IoT system.

2. *Local communications:* These are the communication channels that employed to support the method of sensor-based device use for communicating with neighbouring devices.

3. *Application protocols:* These are the designed frameworks that specify the method how information content should be transmitted.

4. *Gateways:* These devices are responsible for translation as well as re-transmission of information, via linking local device networks to the internet.

5. *Network servers:* The network servers are the systems responsible for managing the acceptance and transmission of IoT data, which are located at cloud data centres.

6. *Cloud applications:* These process IoT data into information, which can be comprehended by the users.

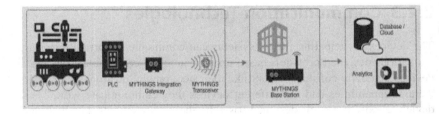

FIGURE 2.3   Workflow of Data from Device to Cloud Databases for Analytics

7. *User interfaces:* These are the components that connect the users, where people can view the IoT information, manipulate it and issue commands back to IoT devices.

2.2.3.2 Internet of Things Devices

IoT devices can be defined as any electronic devices that are capable of communicating via internet as shown in Figure 2.3. In this chapter we focus on those devices that are used to control the lights or check tank levels for manufacturing of chemicals. Two of the examples are Digi XBee for industrial tank sensors and Digi ConnectCore System on Module (SOM).

2.2.3.3 Connecting Wireless Devices

The majority of the electronics devices created were regular devices that did not have any internet capabilities. Hence, they had to be modified with aftermarket solutions in order to attain connecting capabilities. However, the new IoT-based devices are currently being built with these features into it along with reduced cost and improved functionality. These devices are customarily developed on the basis of the application but fundamentally carry few features like:

- Sensor with the feature of detecting physical occurrences, like motion or a water leak.
- Actuators designed that perhaps could also create physical changes, such as turning on a light or closing a valve.
- Sensors and actuators inscribed with one or more microprocessors executing the logic that could drive the IoT functionality.
- All connected devices are designed typically with at least one communication component, either some kind of radio or certain wired communication mode like Ethernet.

- IoT devices are usually battery operated, which can make power management a primary consideration during the process of selecting equipment, designing functionality and creating communications strategies.

2.2.3.4 Local Communication Methods and Protocols

All devices participating in the IoT systems need to mandatorily communicate, as information sender or as information receiver or as both. Certain communications with the peer devices are directly delivered to the receiver, whereas in others, it passes via gateways to the destination.

Here the graphical model for wireless communication illustrates the defined role of each node in the network with respect to the network topology. The "star network" shown in Figure 2.4A, represents a smart wireless module that coordinates communications to the intermediate devices that act as routers, and they move the communications out to other end devices.

As the combination of electronic devices, their positions and the topology change, so as change the wireless devices architecture, their communication medium and protocols.

The following examples show the diagram (Figure 2.4B), representing how networks can be built to behave in a variety of ways with the use of divergent wireless protocols. The quality of protocol is dominated by factors such as distance between communicating nodes within the network.

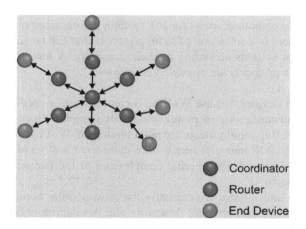

FIGURE 2.4A   Star Network Topology

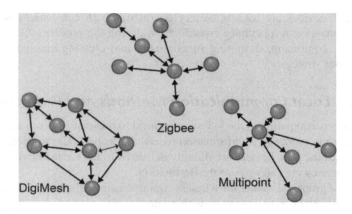

FIGURE 2.4B   Various Wireless Protocols

The initial hop in IoT communication may be either wired or wireless where wired connections may use simple serial protocols for communication. However, a direct networking system like Ethernet is typically used for allowing direct internet protocol (TCP/IP) connections to a network server or cloud application. The messages that are transmitted over the internet are typically routed via various devices, which are concealed easily and safely by IoT devices. Though wired networks are fast where cables are good carriers of electricity and signals, they are expensive and quite impractical to execute the system via physical systems.

The wireless communications for IoT systems are designed over radio signals; hence, there is a collection of radio protocols that can be adopted by the communication systems according to their suitability. A few of the popular communication protocols are discussed as follows:

- Certain devices that use Wi-Fi as a communication medium prove quite advantageous in power, unless its complex processing and provisioning requirements are not a hindrance. Wi-Fi protocol executes TCP/IP natively; hence once completed with configuration, it can hide away the internal complexities of the internet running underneath.
- Zigbee and Z-wave are currently the most popular home automation networking protocol designing and developing organizations as they are optimized for low-power, low-bandwidth communications, and both allow devices in the home front for direct interaction among devices for meeting speed and security requirements. Both

the protocols provide direct support for internet protocol, so communications beyond the local area are typically routed via gateway.

- LoRaWAN protocol is also quite popular for providing low-bandwidth-enabled IoT services as well. It typically combines long ranges with very low bandwidth, which can support line-of-sight range for devices that are spread out through miles of distances.
- Bluetooth and its low-energy sister, BLE, are one of the few extremely popular simple IoT devices. These devices generally do not support long-distance communication; hence, often a mobile phone is used to support long-distance messaging.
- Cellular networks are currently capable of easily accommodating IoT devices. Various new cellular protocols such as Cat-M and NB-IoT allow battery-operated devices to run for months without undergoing any recharging for very limited bandwidth.
- A few other protocols like 4G LTE and 5G call for more power but may also handle heavy data like digital videos.
- There are quite many proprietaries with single-manufacturer protocols that are tuned for distance-based needs, with special bandwidth requirements, difficult radio environments and, of course, cost optimization. One cannot identify a protocol that can rule them all. Every project carries their own best solution.

The various frameworks capturing computer network-based applications or protocols are defined and structured in virtual layers called the "OSI networking model" as shown in Figure 2.5. The OSI model or Open Systems Interconnection model can be described as the conceptual framework where the components or the individual layers of the network operate. The lowest layer of the model deals with the physical part, wires or the radio waves. The next layers typically coordinate the message formation.

The topmost layer takes care of the useful content under transmission and is also called the "application layer." This layer is mainly responsible for all communication-related activities within the network.

Considering the heterogenous nature of the devices participating in Green/General IoT, there is a need of standardization over the details regarding communication protocols and implementation details.

A few of the standardized application protocols that provide a standard language format are Zigbee, Bluetooth and Z-Wave, which include all application protocols that generally provide a standard language, for example, a light switch designed and developed by one company is capable to turn on three different lamps made by a single company.

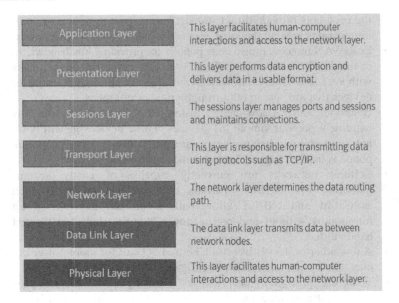

FIGURE 2.5   Layers of OSI Model for Networking Protocol

Some application protocols are quite generic in application, e.g., MQTT and CoAP, where both are technically lightweight application protocols, which standardize the communication modes and channels between technically different devices without restrictions over messages. Being lightweight, these protocols occupy quite low bandwidth and thus very little power, making them ideal for electronic devices that are battery operated.

The typical electronic devices that offer more power and bandwidth may employ a restful communication through HTTP protocol, which in fact is the protocol working for the web. The framework of HTTP is quite a task agnostic but has a drawback of draining out both bandwidth and battery of small IoT devices and hence needs attention while implementation.

2.2.3.5 Gateways

While IoT system participating devices lack the capability of running a TCP/IP protocol directly, it has the option of passing the message to another device via gateways.

Gateway takes the responsibility of processing and forwarding the messages to and from the internet.

Gateways are the electronic devices that are designed and implemented in an IoT-based system with the perspective of helping to maintain small battery-operated and inexpensive devices. Gateways typically handle multiple devices as local base stations. A few examples based on some real-life scenarios are as follows:

- Many wearable devices that execute Bluetooth/BLE commonly use a mobile phone as their gateway to the internet. It offers a good solution for the systems that are built upon the phone and the devices that are geographically located nearby each other.
- Multiple home automation protocols such as Zigbee, Z-Wave and LoRaWAN are difficult to handle via mobile phones directly, due to their mobile nature. Such protocols may make use of a gateway box, which is generally plugged into wall power and Ethernet, Wi-Fi or cellular. Such systems typically receive information from devices via their native protocols, such as Zigbee, which first process what they receive and thereafter forward it over the internet.
- Certain industrial applications such as solar fields and wind fields need a robust industrial gateway to route communications to and from devices that are distributed across the remote device network, as shown in Figure 2.6.

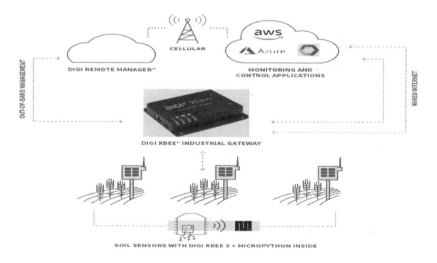

FIGURE 2.6 Gateways for Various Application Protocols

Their devices with low capacity of performing as a gateway can also support communication via multi-hop gateway process, which allows devices with limited capabilities to connect with far-off locations. The process often utilizes a series of divergent protocols to get the job done. These gateways, in general, use application protocols, e.g., MQTT, REST or CoAP, to connect with a network server or cloud application.

2.2.3.6 Network Servers and Cloud Applications

The majority of IoT-based communications are addressed by certain network-based servers as shown in Figure 2.7. These protocols are typically usable in areas pertaining to completion of low-level work or de-duplication of redundant messages as well as conversion of specific protocol formats. The protocol does not need any additional processing but is quite helpful for communication and configuration management as well as maintaining the security and providing the report over the devices themselves.

Most IoT communications are initially accepted and handled by some type of network server. Certain protocols require this to complete low-level work like de-duplication of redundant messages and conversion of special protocol formats. Even when a protocol does not require additional processing, it is endlessly helpful to have a system that not only manages communications but can also configure, secure and report over the devices themselves.

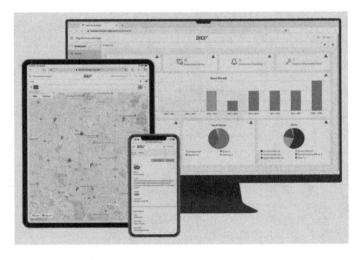

FIGURE 2.7   Network Servers to Handle IoT Communications
Source: https://www.digi.com/blog/post/how-do-iot-devices-communicate

Currently in market, Digi Remote Manager can serve as one of the examples that dominate the industry for applications pertaining to cloud-based services. Other services like AWS and Azure also provide IoT-based data processing as an additional feature with certain generic device management techniques. These systems may collaborate together to provide reference to customer-based relations.

The IoT data once being operated upon by network servers is thereafter exchanged with the cloud application, which would further process the data into useful information for further analysis.

The cloud-based applications are often executed in parallel with other network services over the same platforms such as AWS, Azure etc. These applications are created using common languages such as Node.js, Python or Java, which are tied to an SQL or NoSQL server capable of managing huge quantities of data coming from fleets of IoT devices. A few of the used cases are as follows:

- The conversion of pulse readings from electric meters into decisions regarding online implementation of power plants.
- Conversion of temperature readings into weather predictions.

Here flow of information is bidirectional; hence, the cloud servers are required to manage critically the outgoing commands, which control the majority of operations ranging from traffic lights to chicken coop feeders.

Even with all of this technology in place, human interaction is always required. So a critical task for cloud servers is providing the user interface that brings people into the loop.

2.2.3.7 User Interface

In the IoT systems, user interface can be considered as the end point in IoT communication chain. They are the starting point in the chain of commands that typically flows through the system of multiple IoT devices for execution.

There are multiple kinds of user interfaces where an IoT solution is generally capable of supporting more than one.

As we know, we humans have a habit of getting connected with the system via multiple devices such as websites, smartphone mobile app, special desktop application or indirectly through an Application Programming Interface (API) integration with business services like Salesforce as shown in Figure 2.7. Many interactions take place over a remote mode, while many via on-board touchscreen or switches. Irrespective of the method considered as the user interface, the focus is all about real usage of their IoT systems and the information they create from it.

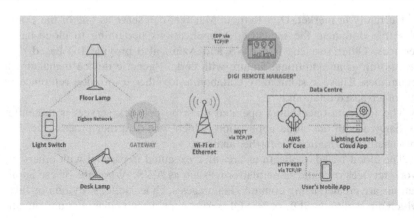

FIGURE 2.8   The Various Zigbee Protocols to Control and Manage Home Automation Systems and Applications
Source: https://www.digi.com/blog/post/how-do-iot-devices-communicate

2.2.4 Use Case: Light Switch

One of the examples is where a homeowner wants to control their dining room lamp via the local switch, where he should be able to flip the lights on and off remotely. They implemented the concept via a system that included a battery-powered IoT wall switch, which was capable of communicating directly with lamps via Zigbee wireless protocol as depicted in Figure 2.8.

The Zigbee protocol as a device includes a feature where it supports specially designed language for lighting purpose. Zigbee as a protocol is technically of low bandwidth, which does not require or use much power and is limited in range. Hence, for all remote access, they require a small gateway device, where the gateway translates Zigbee messages into the MQTT application protocol and passes it over to the network and cloud server that will be executing the home automation system application. The cloud application thereafter reverts back to the homeowner via the mobile app. Using the app, the owner can access and view the current state of the dining room light irrespective of their geographic location.

2.3 COMPUTATION

In many of the IoT-based applications, the focus is more over data gathering, which may subsequently be processed and visualized. These computations are applicable in general based on metrics such as CPU or network load. This clearly indicates that a significant quantity of data is required to be transmitted over the network via Network File system. This makes the data to be available to the node that is responsible for its processing.

2.4 SERVICES: THE INTERNET OF THINGS

IoT-based services represent a set of end-to-end services designed by an enterprise as a contract with external providers such as designing, building, installing and operating the IoT solutions. Some of the services may also include advisory consulting for IoT planning and much more. The IoT service providers typically include a range of small, midsize as well as large service firms, which are capable for building as well as deploying the IoT solution applications across a wide range of industries.

The market here concentrates over the medium as well as the large-scale service providing sectors that support the key vertical markets for the IoT adoption. A few examples of such sectors are the manufacturing industry, healthcare sectors, transportation and retail. The current market trends are more aligned towards designing, building as well as installing the IoT-based solution systems, which include planning services for IoT-enabled digital business environment.

Ranging over various sectors of our lives, be it industry, enterprise or domestic, IoT has found applications in almost every area that has the capability of connecting everything with everyone. The concept of IoT has made the world smarter and ever more promising towards improvising the quality of life ever before. Advent of new IoT-enabled devices and coming up of new IoT-based designs with respect to concepts like smart city, smart machines and Industry 4.0 have made the IoT concept quite sought after and all the more innovative. A few enterprises have facilitated transforming the business needs for organizations into competitive differentiators by delivering innovative IoT-powered solutions. A few of the innovative services that can be considered are as follows:

- Analyse and act over new data collected over IoT-based devices.
- Integration and transformation of business processes.
- Improving the decision making with augmented intelligence aided by IoT.
- Designing, developing, integrating, deploying and managing end-to-end IoT processes.
- Seamless integration of IoT solutions with business architecture.

2.5 SEMANTICS

Currently, modern IoT systems are composed of various subsystems, which generally require interaction among them to be performed in a horizontal manner. This composition poses quite a challenge with respect to maintaining interoperability among the participating devices.

The semantic interoperability may be defined as the aggregation of technologies, which supports the computer systems into interacting in an unambiguous manner. This method is quite suitable for being implemented in order to lower the cost of integrated subsystems while being quite futuristic in approach. This is one of the core requirements for designing as well as implementing autonomous operations in IoT-based systems for Industry 4.0.

The semantic interoperability has currently improved the ability of conceiving and building systems that are IoT based in nature.

The section deals with the concept of semantic interoperability and the huge range of opportunities it creates.

The semantic interoperability concept can even be implemented today via various declarative models as well as logic statements, also called semantic models, which provide a masking of the formal vocabulary of a certain kind.

The core purpose of providing such structured semantic models is that they would support unambiguous understanding of other such subsystems using the same mechanism. Here, the clear conceptualization may be treated as the cornerstone for other subsystems in order to perform a confident interaction with respect to understand the information received as well as provide commands to share information to and fro with other subsystems to achieve certain output.

The concept of interoperability is not just restricted to understanding and exchange of formats or translation of any given information models to be communicated between a producer and a consumer. Rather it focuses more on enabling the entire process as an automated procedure without being explicitly programmed or fully machine processable.

The current industry standards have greatly improvised the interoperability concept, which has remarkably reduced the efforts involved. This change has been brought about by standardization of vocabulary and concepts.

These standards enjoy quite an attention within an industry or technical vertical for subsystems within a given system. Designing the concept of horizontal interoperability that would mandate the transparency among other participating systems exchanges communication messages with a given system. This issue is currently the fundamental challenge that is being addressed by semantic interoperability, which also has been mandated as a norm in the IoT world, where new applications will be put together in the same systems where each will be developed independently and for their purpose.

2.5.1 The Importance of the Role of Semantic Interoperability in Internet of Things

The concept of semantic interoperability is about the ability to initiate the concerted meaning of the data under consideration to be exchanged along with the ability to comprehend the communication interfaces in a similar fashion. The shared concept here indicates two separate computers that would interpret the data in the same manner apart from communicating the considered data in its basic sense.

The design and building of the IoT-based systems pose a lot of challenges with respect to the scaling factors as well as ensuring that equipment, electronic devices and subsystems designed and developed by different vendors is interoperable. These systems are also expected to operate over different time periods as and when required. The different designed internet protocol suites (IP, TCP/UDP, HTTP/CoAP etc.) as shown in Figure 2.9 have performed well being integrated with various device architecture. However, the subsystems are all equipped with their specific information model, data model, syntactic flavour and concepts, which cause a different kind of barrier at a higher level while integrating subsystems coming from multiple vendors.

Apart from the challenge of holding the core semantic interoperability, these systems also deal with the issue of maintaining and preserving the exact concise meaning and significance of a piece of data across different domains.

The reducing of interoperability component among subsystems results in heavy time consumption, is expensive and is prone to errors. In such system configurations, the major challenge and focus are about integration and

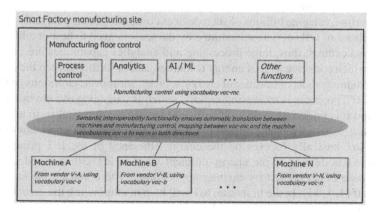

FIGURE 2.9   Interconnected Things in a Smart Factory Enabling High-Level Interoperability
Source: https://www.ericsson.com/en/blog/2020/7/semantic-interoperability-in-iot

maintenance of these systems. Here a major focus and efforts are spent over the manual contribution, which probably is difficult to automate due to the varying interpretation of humans for the involved data.

2.6 CONCEPT OF GREEN INTERNET OF THINGS

The persistent popularity of IoT has made the concept break through every domain of technology in various fields, i.e., commercial, industrial and domestic fronts. IoT involved internet-controlled devices are being used everywhere. Some of the applications with extensive use of IoT are Paper Application [3], Food Supply Chain [4], Mining Industry [4], Transportation Industry [5], Garments Industry [6], Smart Cities [7] and Smart Homes. According to the various experiments and testingon the IoT-based electronic devices, all devices are equipped with radio frequency identification (RFID), which requires a small quantity of power to operate. Based on their functionality, active RFIDs are indeed necessary for effective services.

Considering the extensive use of IoT and IoT-based devices, the amount of energy that is being consumed regularly for transmission of data is generated in huge quantities by the various sensor devices to huge data centres, which requires heavy processing along with strong analytical capabilities. The entire process involves robust computation as well as processing, ending up consuming a huge amount of power. To add it all, there is dearth of energy for regular traditional machines or cvx.

Therefore, imagine billions of such devices consuming energy on daily basis, and millions of GBs of data transmitted by the sensors need to best or edited by huge data centres; thus, huge processing and analytics capabilities are needed [8–9], which consume a lot of energy resources, and to further deepen the crisis, we are running short of traditional energy sources. Moreover, emissions of CO_2 due to ICT products is increasing rapidly, which is damaging our environment [10], and it is projected to do so if sufficient measures are not taken to address this concern. To solve these critical problems, Green IoT is an important topic. Green IoT basically focuses on the energy efficiency of the IoT principles. Green IoT is defined as the energy-efficient ways in IoT either to reduce the greenhouse effect caused by existing applications or to eradicate the same in IoT itself [1, 5, 11]. In the first case, IoT will help in eliminating the greenhouse effect, but in the second scenario, the IoT will be further optimized to stop the greenhouse effect. Every step in IoT should be made green, from design to implementation. In order to implement the Green IoT, a number of strategies should be adopted. Various technological solutions for Green IoT have been proposed [4]. The details of these strategies will be discussed in later sections, but a brief summary is provided in this section. For implementation of Green IoT, a framework was proposed by Bedi et al. [12] for the energy-efficient optimization of IoT objects. Furthermore, Green IoT may be implemented by using green RFIDs, green data centres [13], green sensor networks [14] and green cloud computing [15–16]. Details of these will be discussed in later sections. IoT is an emerging technology that is changing the way we see the IT industry. IoT is going to have a huge impact on how we deal with certain problems in our daily life, and it is certainly going to make our lives easier and better, but with ease come the challenges. We have to deal with the large-scale consumption of energy resources by IoT, and the earlier we tackle this problem, the more efficient will be the IoT.

2.7 LAYERED ARCHITECTURE OF GREEN INTERNET OF THINGS

This section presents the layered architecture of IoT indicating the power-hungry components in each layer. This layered architecture aims to achieve ubiquity and pervasiveness in IoT systems by sensing, analysing, communicating and processing of large data [17]. It is a mixture of hardware and software technologies, communication protocols and different processing technologies. The existing architectures vary with application domain and design, QoS factors, interoperability etc. It also emphasizes on the major power-hungry nodes, protocols, middleware elements and applications. The architecture is divided into five layers: Perception, Transport, Processing, Network and Application as shown in Figure 2.10. The components associated with every layer is shown in Figure 2.11. These components are segregated into power-hungry and non-power-hungry components.

| Perception Layer |
| Transport Layer |
| Processing Layer |
| Network Layer |
| Application Layer |

FIGURE 2.10   Layered Architecture of IoT [18–19]

a. *Perception layer:* This layer senses data and provides scheduling and communication with other sensors. The major tasks of this layer are self-organized sensing and load balancing. The components of this layer include sensors, RFID, sink nodes, actuators, gateway nodes and software solutions (application like bootstrap software) of which sink nodes, gateway nodes, actuators and passive RFID are power hungry [3, 5]. The examples of sensors are medical, military, chemical, ADC, accelerometers, camera, GPS etc. [20].

b. *Transport layer:* This layer serves as a pipe for transferring data from perception to processing layer. The components of this layer include 3G, LAN, Bluetooth, RFID, NFC, Wi-Fi, etc., of which NFC, Wi-Fi, coordinators, trust centre gateway and master-slave Bluetooth model are power-hungry components [17]. The examples of transport layer components are tags, reader, electrometers, short range communication protocols, trust centre, gateway etc. [20].

c. *Processing/Middleware layer:* In this layer, a large amount of data is analysed, processed and stored. This layer provides services to the lower layers, allocates resources for efficient storage in virtual and physical machines and converts the data into required form. The components of this layer include processing elements, middleware and databases, of which the processing elements such as virtual machines, resource allocator, data centres, analytic centre and information convertor are power-hungry components [16].

The examples of processing elements are online servers, data centres, microcontrollers, microprocessors, etc., while the examples of middleware are semantic-based and service-based middleware, event-based and process-oriented middleware, Contiki, TinyOS, RTOS and databases such as data warehouses and allocator CPU.

d. *Network layer:* This layer provides communication between devices of other layers as a whole system model. The components of this layer include WSN nodes, cloud servers and big data gateway nodes of which WSN nodes, base stations, big data centres and routing gateway nodes are power-hungry components [16]. The examples of WSN elements are low-power devices, sensing, computing, power and routing components, hubs and switches, IoT cellular operators and remote transmitting nodes, and examples of cloud servers are WebBroker and virtual devices [18].

e. *Application layer:* This is an abstract layer for the users to avail services of the lower layers [21]. It provides the visualization of processed data in the form of intelligent tasks. Examples of the applications include smart homes, smart buildings, smart vehicles, healthcare, smart environment, supply chain management, energy conservation, etc., of which control systems usually are power-hungry appliances.

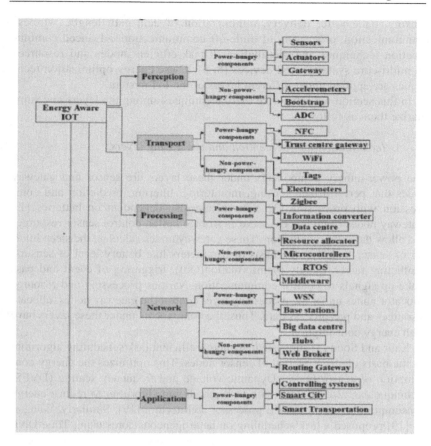

FIGURE 2.11   Classification of IoT Components

2.8 ENERGY OPTIMIZATION TECHNIQUES IN INTERNET OF THINGS TECHNOLOGIES

Primarily, energy is consumed by various tasks such as sensing, communicating, processing and actuating within and across the layers. The overall architectural elements communicate with each other and thus consume more energy.

Some of the principles on which energy-efficient technologies are proposed in the literature include sleep-off scheduling mechanisms and selective sensing, data buffer delivery, minimization of data path length, wireless communication, processing of trade-off communication, advanced communication techniques and distribution of task-efficient nodes and resources on multi-core system based devices [8, 3]. These energy optimization techniques are applied under different layers of the IoT system. In this section we categorize these techniques among the layers and summarize them as follows.

a. *Techniques under perception and processing layers:*

The power-hungry components under these layers are sensor and gateway nodes that perform data sensing, monitoring, filtering, prediction and compression with processing. [3]. Sensors are also dependent on batteries [1]. Gateway nodes (relay nodes) serve as storage buffer, control sensor resources and allow data communication. These gateway nodes calculate the sleep interval of sensor nodes on the basis of parameters like battery level of sensors, conflicting factor, quality of information(QoI), triggering of event and pass wake-up signals to control communication. Various processing and resource allocator nodes under the processing layer control the gateway nodes, allocate resources and pre-process data. Thus, the components under these layers have high energy consumption.

Kaur and Sood [3] suggested an energy-efficient task scheduling algorithm on the basis of sleep interval of sensor nodes. This optimizes the energy consumption of sensor nodes. Dynamic voltage and frequency scaling (DVFS) technique can also be used with task scheduling algorithm to reduce energy consumption of BIG.LITTLE processor architecture [19]. Similarly, Wang et al. [19] proposed a task scheduling on heterogeneous cores using Time Division Multiple Access (TDMA). The selective and compressive sensing technique proposed by Arshad et al. [4] optimizes energy. Other techniques such as QoI-based sensor to task duty cycle allocation [5] and selective and compressive sensing [4] also optimize energy consumption of sensor and gateway nodes. There exists few energy-efficient techniques at the processing layer, such as allocation of server and workload distribution at data centres [1], varied power down mechanisms [6] and cooperation among the nodes while processing [8, 19].

b. *Techniques under transport and network layers:*

These layers address wireless sensing and networking aspects such as routing, servicing of requests and data communication mechanisms. They also include functionalities like transmission of data, neighbourhood communication, retransmission and avoidance of packet collision and hand-shaking mechanisms [22]. These communication mechanisms consume a lot of energy. In addition, in network transmissions, location information in routing, interoperability of heterogeneous things and massive data movement consume more power [23]. With the immense hike in users and application providers, there is an increase in network traffic resulting in high energy consumption. In WSN, network sensor nodes and communication units transmit information for a large period of time resulting in high energy consumption [24, 18].

The energy optimization techniques proposed in [18] include multi-hop and cooperative multi-hop routing in WSN communication to base stations. These techniques route the changing data on the hop-to-hop level, thus reducing the energy consumed in long path transmission. Another technique proposed by Oteafy et al. [25] is based on parallel communication among the sensors and pruning of network requests using Pruned Adaptive Routing protocol. This technique provides optimized routes to the target node, thereby effectively reducing energy consumption. There are few optimization techniques that work on hubs and switches to minimize the path length in data transmission.

c. *Techniques under application layers:*

Applications that actuate the process and display the output are highly battery constrained. Any web application, mobile sensors, actuators and control systems like HVAC have high computations since they perform the tasks like content management, web and directory services etc. Data processing on the basis of HTTP consumes power because of verbosity and large parsing overhead. Such compute-intensive and high-performance appliances consume more energy at the application layer.

There are various energy optimization techniques existing in the literature at this layer. Datta et al. [10] surveyed machine learning algorithms to predict energy consumption by detecting various activities in the applications.

The different energy optimization techniques addressed in this layer include Message Queue Telemetry Transport (MQTT) and Constrained Application Protocol (CoAP), CoAP as an alternative to HTTP, tracking mechanism and MQTT-S/MQTT-SN [24]. In IoT systems, applications like smart cities use technologies such as distributed control and fog computing that create a dynamic and distributed energy control framework. Also, techniques like mass transit gain more merit in terms of larger capacity, higher delivery efficiency, lower energy consumption and costs [22].

2.9 ISSUES AND CHALLENGES

Although there exist a lot of research papers on IoT systems, researchers are still focusing on identifying the power-hungry components/aspects in IoT systems and are working on optimization solutions. Some of the research efforts made by existing researchers are described in this book. There still exist technical challenges which are listed next [26–28]:

1. Design of energy-efficient elements at the processing layer is required to be addressed as most of these processing elements consume lot of energy in storing, managing and processing of a large amount of data.
2. In the perception layer, sensors should be made energy efficient due to high power consumption in continuous sensing mechanism.
3. Continual sensing, controlling by gateway, processing by data centres and processors, network transmission and long running applications are challenging in these devices as more energy is consumed by these devices.
4. Also, huge numbers of things interact at these layers via a large amount of real-time data, interoperability and intelligent processes that need to be considered to make energy-efficient systems [29, 30].

2.10 CONCLUSION

The chapter has discussed a number of Green IoT devices, green components and participating elements with their architectural background. The chapter highlights the concept of green in the devices and its impact on society and the environment and strategies that could be adopted in order to implement a green system as a whole. The chapter also highlights the architectural layers and details their implementation with the interoperability requirements and finally states challenges and issues that are currently being faced while implementing the concept in practice, opening few of the research areas to be adopted hereafter.

REFERENCES

[1] K. Wang, et al. "Green Industrial Internet of Things Architecture: An Energy-Efficient Perspective," *IEEE Communications Magazine*, vol. 54, no. 12, pp. 48–54, 2016.

[2] J. Gubbi, et al., "Internet of Things (IoT): A Vision, Architectural Elements, and Future Directions," *Future Generation Computer Systems*, vol. 29, no. 7, pp. 1645–1660, 2013.

[3] N. Kaur, S.K. Sood, "An Energy-Efficient Architecture for the Internet of Things (IoT)," *IEEE Systems Journal*, vol. 11, no. 2, pp. 796–805, 2017.

[4] R. Arshad, et al., "Green IoT: An Investigation on Energy Saving Practices for 2020 and Beyond," *IEEE Access*, vol. 5, pp. 15667–15681, 2017.

[5] L. Atzori, A. Iera, G. Morabito, "The Internet of Things: A Survey," *Computer Networks*, vol. 54, no. 15, pp. 2787–2805, 2010.

[6] D. Jiang, et al., "Energy-Efficient Multi-Constraint Routing Algorithm With Load Balancing for Smart City Applications," *IEEE Internet of Things Journal*, vol. 3, no. 6, pp. 1437–1447, 2016.

[7] T. Qiu, et al., "A Task-Efficient Sink Node Based on Embedded Multi-Core soC for Internet of Things," *Future Generation Computer Systems*, vol. 82, pp. 656–666, 2016.

[8] S.F. Abedin, et al., "A System Model for Energy Efficient Green-IoT Network," *Event 2015 International Conference on Information Networking, ICOIN 2015 –* Siem Reap, Cambodia.

[9] M. Aazam, P.P. Hung, E.-N. Huh, "Smart Gateway based Communication for Cloud of Things," *Intelligent Sensors, Sensor Networks and Information Processing (ISSNIP), IEEE Ninth International Conference*, Singapore, 2014.

[10] S.K. Datta, et al., "Web of Things for Connected Vehicles," *25th International World Wide Web Conference*, 2016.

[11] A. Bagula, L. Castelli, M. Zennaro, "On the Design of Smart Parking Networks in the Smart Cities: An Optimal Sensor Placement Model," *Sensors*, vol. 15, no. 7, pp. 15443–15467, 2015.

[12] G. Bedi, G.K. Venayagamoorthy, R. Singh, "Internet of Things (IoT) Sensors for Smart Home Electric Energy Usage Management," *Information and Automation for Sustainability (ICIAfS) 2016 IEEE International Conference on*, Galle, Sri Lanka, pp. 1–6, 2016.

[13] Y.-K. Chen, "Challenges and Opportunities of Internet of Things," *Design Automation Conference (ASP-DAC), 2012 17th Asia and South Pacific*, Sydney, Australia, 2012.

[14] K. Georgiou, S. Xavier-de-Souza, K. Eder., "The IoT Energy Challenge: A Software Perspective," *IEEE Embedded Systems Letters*, vol. 10, no. 3, pp. 53–56, 2017.

[15] H. Jayakumar, et al., "Energy-Efficient System Design for IoT Devices," *Design Automation Conference (ASP-DAC), 21st Asia and South Pacific, IEEE*, Macao, China, 2016. DOI: 10.1109/ASPDAC.2016.7428027.

[16] C. Zhu, et al., "Green Internet of Things for Smart World," *IEEE Access*, vol. 3, pp. 2151–2162, 2015.

[17] A. Whitmore, A. Agarwal, L. Da Xu., "The Internet of Things—A survey of Topics and Trends," *Information Systems Frontiers*, vol. 17, no. 2, pp. 261–274, 2015.

[18] P. Sethi, S.R. Sarangi, "Internet of Things: Architectures, Protocols, and Applications," *Journal of Electrical and Computer Engineering*, vol. 2017, 2017. Article ID 9324035, https://doi.org/10.1155/2017/9324035.

[19] Z. Wang, et al., "An Energy-Efficient Heterogeneous Dual-core Processor for Internet of Things," *Circuits and Systems (ISCAS), IEEE International Symposium on*, IEEE, Institute of Electrical and Electronics Engineers, Lisbon, Portugal, 2015.

[20] Á. Asensio, et al., "Protocol and Architecture to Bring Things Into Internet of Things," *International Journal of Distributed Sensor Networks*, vol. 10, no. 4, pp. 158–252, 2014.

[21] K.K. Patil, S.M. Patel, "Internet of Things-IOT: Definition, Characteristics, Architecture, Enabling Technologies, Application & Future Challenges," *International Journal of Engineering Science and Computing*, vol. 6, no. 5, 2016.

[22] Y. Wang, H. Qi, "Research of Intelligent Transportation System Based on the Internet of Things Frame," *Journal of Wireless Engineering and Technology*, vol. 3, no. 03, p. 160, 2012.

[23] A. Gaur, et al., "Smart City Architecture and Its Applications based on IoT," *Procedia Computer Science*, vol. 52, pp. 1089–1094, 2015.

[24] M. Vellanki, S.P.R. Kandukuri, A. Razaque, "Node Level Energy Efficiency Protocol for Internet of Things," *Journal of Theoretical and Computational Science*, vol. 3, 2016.

[25] S.M.A. Oteafy, F.M. Al-Turjman, H.S. Hassanein, "Pruned Adaptive Routing in the Heterogeneous Internet of Things," *IEEE Global Communications Conference (GLOBECOM)*, Springer International Publishing, Switzerland, 2012.

[26] R. Coppola, M. Morisio., "Connected Car: Technologies, Issues, Future Trends," *ACM Computing Surveys (CSUR)*, vol. 49, no. 3, p. 46, 2016.

[27] W. Ejaz, et al., "Efficient Energy Management for the Internet of Things in Smart Cities," *IEEE Communications Magazine*, vol. 55, no. 1, pp. 84–91, 2017.

[28] S. Rani, et al., "A Novel Scheme for an Energy Efficient Internet of Things based on Wireless Sensor Networks," *Sensors*, vol. 15, no. 11, pp. 28603–28626, 2015.

[29] M. Wu, et al., "Research on the Architecture of Internet of Things," *Advanced Computer Theory and Engineering (ICACTE), 3rd IEEE International Conference, Chengdu,* vol. 5, 2010.

[30] L. Da Xu, W. He, S. Li., "Internet of Things in Industries: A Survey," *IEEE Transactions on Industrial Informatics*, vol. 10, no. 4, pp. 2233–2243, 2014.

Advanced Computing for Green Internet of Things

3

3.1 INTRODUCTION

The concept of Internet of Things (IoT) prevailing all over the world has contributed immensely to establishing a global connectivity over the physical object scattered worldwide. The world is currently seen to be leveraging heavily over the recent advancements in the field of science and technology, which makes the world a smart place to live in with people collaborating automatically with heterogeneous devices. The amount of huge data and information flowing within these connecting devices to make an interactive system ends up consuming huge quantities of energy [1]. The traditional IoT systems are interconnected to huge databases and warehouses to facilitate multiple operations such as big data analytics, enable cloud computing or predict smart device behaviour, extract useful business insights, provide feedback control and many more. Multiple commercial enterprises and multi-national companies have adapted to the rising interest of smart world, resulting in a rapid increase in demand of energy from these sectors [2–3]. If considered worldwide requirement of power, it will be true to state that, increase in number of commercial ventures, has ended up with a never-ending surge for technological requirements. The concept of Green IoT is all about reducing the environmental issues and thereby building a sustainable environment related to IoT [4]. It has been thereafter highlighted by the scientists that usage of energy-efficient technologies in IoT either reduces the impact of greenhouse gases or

DOI: 10.1201/9781003204503-3

inhibits the greenhouse effect in various IoT applications. The system assists in maintaining the climate by using low-energy consumption devices or electrical appliances, minimizing greenhouse gas emissions, utilizing carbon-free materials and promoting reusability [5]. The chapter discusses in brief the aspects of advanced computing concepts such as smart sensor objects, green data centres, sensor network and cloud computing, which play a major role in controlling the environmental effects of traditional IoT for saving energy [6].

3.2 SMART OBJECTS IN GREEN INTERNET OF THINGS

Similar research on IoT architectures has highlighted the potentialities that are significantly curbed out owing to the limitations imposed by the dichotomy exhibited by RFID nature, i.e., simple radio frequency identification (RFID) tags or networked RFID readers [7–8]. Currently, a large amount of research is being conducted in order to overcome this restriction. Some studies [9–11] have shown various alternatives proposed by researchers working towards designing alternative architectural models for the IoT that are loosely coupled, decentralized systems of smart objects. These are the autonomous physical/ digital objects capable of sensing, processing, acting as well as performing various network-related activities.

As compared to passive RFID tags, some smart objects carry huge data bytes, which are technically the chunks of application logic, which support the device in grasping the local scenario while interacting with human users as well as other smart objects located nearby [12]. These objects sense, log and interpret the changes they are undergoing including places around there close proximity that impact them in certain way. They intercommunicate within each other, exchange information along with people around and try to collect information regarding facts such as their geographic locations, other objects in their vicinity and their own historical data related to their past.

The idea of smart objects and IoT has been recently publicized by Sterling [9], where he coined the term "spime" that describes the whole concept of space-time, action-aware, environment-aware, self-logging, self-documenting and uniquely identified objects. These objects are designed to provide data captured with respect to themselves as well as their surroundings [13]. As expressed in the article, the object itself can be tracked down from the point of its inception without any physical existence via its pioneer. It can be tracked down to the extent of its ownership history, its physical location, into its eventual obsolescence as well as its breaking down back into raw material for building further new instantiations of objects.

Chen et al. [9] described the concept of IoT as a combination of smart objects, which may grasp the environment to its fullest and react to it.

With the experience collected via practical experimentation as well as building prototype of some generations of smart objects, authors have been able to identify three categories of smart object types [14]:

- Activity-aware objects,
- Policy-aware objects and
- Process-aware objects.

They have also identified the smart-object design space, as a space of three-dimensional criteria, i.e., awareness, representation and interaction. Ge et al. [11] designed a framework for building the smart objects. An artifact framework has been exclusively designed to represent smart objects along with a pervasive application model to leverage the services of smart objects dynamically.

The same concept was applied by Zheng et al. [12], where the developers were allowed to incorporate heterogeneous physical sensing devices and its applications via providing easy-to-use web service interfaces with the purpose of controlling all kinds of physical sensor devices irrespective of the in-built network technology. The concept incorporates various means for device service discovery, semantic model-driven architecture and security aspects.

A similar design was conceived and proposed by researchers called Libeum World as shown in Figure 3.1, which comprises smart cities integrated with IoT-based applications. The changes that are being brought about by the advent of IoT into industry are quite evident, which confirms it all the more that IoT is undoubtedly the next technological revolution. Though IoT currently seems to be used in every phase of our day-to-day lives, it is still at its infancy stage with respect to its overall possible deployment [16]. The key challenges that need attention here are battery life [15, 17, 18], which is the oxygen factor within the nodes; technological simplicity [14, 19], prevailing the data and context awareness among the nodes in the network [20]; and last but not the least are the privacy and security concerns [21–22], multiple active things and interference-free connectivity, the cost of terminal devices [23], scalability and heterogeneous terminal devices matter [24]. Currently, IoT may be considered as an ecosystem that is tightly coupled with respect to transmission via network for sending and receiving of data. They are quite interconnected as well

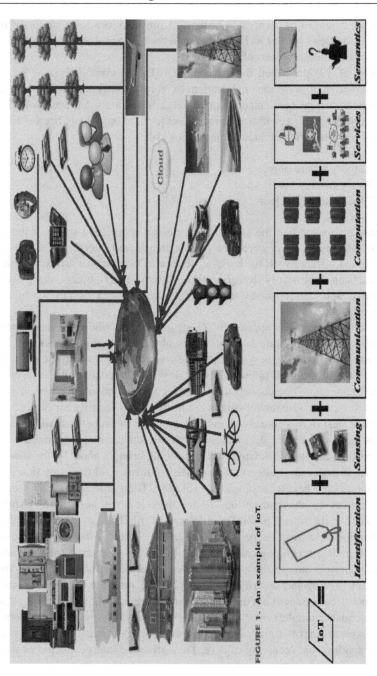

FIGURE 1 - An example of IoT.

FIGURE 3.1 Libeum World: Classic Example of IoT Connecting Heterogeneous Devices Together

as tightly coupled with respect to big data and cloud computing, which makes the system quite intelligent.

3.3 CLOUD COMPUTING FOR GREEN INTERNET OF THINGS

The concept of cloud computing is currently quite useful as well as a popular technique in the current scenario. It is quite a promising technology that offers the whole of computing in the form of utility [1]. The technology supports access of data, software, storage services as well as computation of various services to consumers through the internet.

Platform as a Service (PaaS), Software as a Service (SaaS) and Infrastructure as a Service (IaaS) are the core three services that are provided by cloud computing to consumers. The technology of cloud computing offers several benefits to the IT-based companies as the organizations do not have to bear the cost of building the hardware and software infrastructure reducing the cost overhead. The raise in demand by consumers for services based on computation has motivated many young entrepreneurs and giant companies to open with ideas related to computing service providers, e.g., IBM, Facebook, Yahoo!, Google, Microsoft, etc., and deploy a large number of data centres across various parts of the world and consume huge quantities of energy [15]. However, the rate of consumption of energy in the information industry is constantly increasing. The overall power consumption of any given data centres in 2012 is 38 Giga Watt (GW), which is about 63% high as compared to the power consumption of 2011 [15]. It was herewith estimated that the overall total power will be enough to meet the energy needs of all residential households of the United Kingdom.

The analysis conducted by many researchers and energy-producing sectors indicates that from 2007 to 2030, there is a chance of a rise in energy consumption up to 76%, of which major contributions can be credited to various data centres. This study may be considered a trigger-causing effect that can give way to reducing the overall energy consumption in clouds.

One of the major concerns other than the previously stated is the continuous rise in carbon emissions into the ecosystem, which is due to the rise in consumption of power by these latest technological events in the field of IT.

As highlighted in Chiang et al. [10], "IT industry which is having both information and communication, seems to produce 2% of global carbon dioxide emission."

Hence, the current need of the hour is to make use of eco-friendly technology and its implementable devices such as "green cloud computing" for reduction of both operational energy consumption costs and the environmental impact.

The concept of green computing is mainly designed with the perspective to increase the use of power consumption and energy efficiency, which minimizes the cost and CO_2 emissions [1].

Green computing refers to the attempts to maximize the use of power consumption and energy efficiency and to minimize the cost and CO_2 emissions [1]. The primary objective is the development of new computing models, computer systems and applications that are low cost and have low energy consumption for green computing [4]. Figure 3.2 gives an idea on the amount of energy consumed and carbon dioxide emissions in a single Google search and the amount of carbon dioxide emissions and energy consumption in one month [15].

The cloud data centres use technology known as virtualization [16], which makes it all the more possible for sharing physical resources on servers between different virtual machines (VMs). This offers the option of providing the flexibility of ability to configure various virtual machines over the same physical machines. Virtual machines can be initiated as well as terminated in dynamically over a single host. Every VM is supported with its own characteristics, which requires different quantities of energy depending on the footprint. The total quantity of carbon footprint of the data centre depends on the overall energy consumption provided by each host.

An idle server needs almost half of power than what it needs during its peak power states. An idle server consumes almost half of the power than its peak power state [16]. It uses typically the dynamic migration of virtual machines, which helps into consolidating the overall workloads over only a few number of machines as well as unused machines, which could be made to run over the low-power mode, which can be turned off or can be operated at a low-performance level, e.g., using dynamic voltage and frequency scaling (DVFS) [17]. Hence, VM allocation and migration techniques may be considered useful for saving energy as well as reducing carbon emission rates.

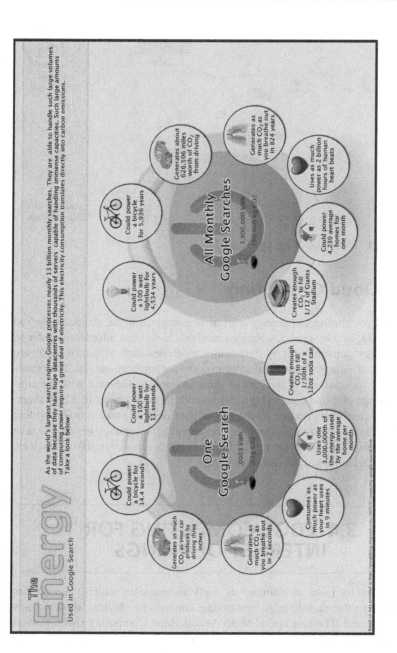

FIGURE 3.2 Energy Consumption in Single Google Search versus Energy Consumption While Conducting Energy Search in a Month

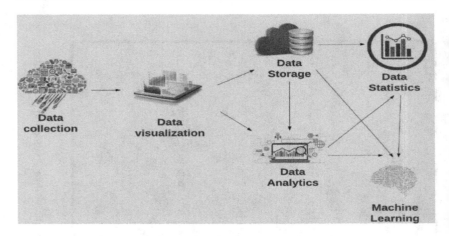

FIGURE 3.3   Overview of IoT Data Analytics

3.3.1 Cloud Computing

The cloud computing technology consumes energy from the data centres and gave out CO_2 as a by-product. Various methods have been adopted in order to lessen energy consumption by data centre machines such as use of hardware virtualization, energy-conversant strap in software applications etc. The ceaseless energy requirement is forecast to show asymptotic increase with the continuous usage of cloud computing services and the data centres that host them. The figures and facts related to the use of data centres make it quite evident that the technology needs to adopt green computing technology in order to save the environment [6]. An overview of IoT data has been collected from devices, processed and analysed, as shown in Figure 3.3.

3.4 EDGE COMPUTING FOR INTERNET OF THINGS

The continuous raise in demand as well as usage of mobile device has given way to the mobile edge computing concept for devices showing low latency demand. The concept of Multi Access Edge Computing (MEC) offers advanced technologies like mobile computing, network congestion control and storage capacity to the edges of the networks. The MEC technology reduces the consumption of mobile energy as well as processes and supports even the critical applications suffering with latency. The popularity of MEC concept was facilitated by 5G technology that combined together both the wireless communication and the mobile computing in order to offload the network computation. The WSN mode is currently carrying out the requirement of sending data by indoor devices, at the front end of Wireless Mesh Sensor Networks (WMSNs). Here the edge devices are deployed to reduce the network congestion that can support the users to tailor their needs via MEC [6].

3.5 SMART WORLD CONTRIBUTION FOR GREEN INTERNET OF THINGS

The huge growth attained in the field of communications as well as sensors and sensor-based devices due to the tremendous development in the domain of telecommunication has successfully connected "things" around us to enable numerous applications and enhance the quality of life [1]. The connectivity implemented among the devices and things in smart cities has been coined as IoT. The IoT technology encompasses various devices in smart cities, capable of being connected anytime, anywhere, via any mode [2–3]. The concept of IoT technology evolves all the more, making the whole IoT concept smart by using adaptive communication network, processing, analysis as well as storage. With respect to the IoT-based context, certain IoT devices include cameras, sensors, radio frequency identification (RFID), actuators, drones, mobile phones etc. All these devices are equipped with the capability to communicate as well as work together in order to reach common goals [1, 4]. Equipped with the capabilities and technological components, the IoT-based devices can be technically used for a broad range of applications, which include real-time monitoring, as seen in environmental monitoring, e-healthcare, transportation autonomy, industry digitalization and automation, home automation etc. The IoT technology is also enabled with software agents that can support sharing of information or make collaborative efforts in implementing some hybrid concept to achieve better results.

The main role of IoT is all about collecting and delivering huge amounts of data pertaining to the advanced communication technologies, which can be analysed for intelligent decision making. The implementation of concepts like big data requirements of IoT requires more storage capacity, cloud computing and wide bandwidth for transmission, in order to make IoT ubiquitous. These big data-processing requirements and transmission of data are few areas that seek to consume high amounts of energy in the IoT devices; hence, uses of efficient and smart techniques are adopted, which could lead to reduced power consumption. The combination of IoT and the practical techniques for lowering the power consumption of big data processing and transmission may immensely contribute to improving the quality of life in smart cities, making the world greener, all the more sustainable and collectively a safer place to live [15–17]. The green and smart cities decrease of pollution hazards and energy demands with efficient resource utilization.

Currently, the smart cities are moving towards adopting the advanced technology that has the potential of modernizing the smart city all the more by use of technologies such as artificial intelligence (AI). Typical examples of this advanced hybrid approach can be found in some smart city technical components such as integrated sensors to create smart transportation systems, incorporating cameras within smart monitoring systems and so on. Some critical aspects of the potential smart cities in 2020, where things or devices were controlled by smart energy management, offered via smart building, smart mobility, smart citizens, smart infrastructure, smart health care, smart technology, smart education and governance etc. These aspects are shown in Figure 3.4.

IoT plays a major role in improving smart cities, refining its numerous applications for enhancing public transformation, reducing traffic congestion, creating cost-effective municipal services, keeping citizens safe and healthier, reducing energy consumption, improving monitoring systems and reducing pollution, as shown in Figure 3.5.

However, IoT-related environmental issues, such as energy consumption, carbon emissions, energy savings, trading, carbon labelling and footprints, have triggered researchers to come up with new solution-based technologies that work towards preserving the environment. Currently, the focus of next-generation technology is on striking a balance between sustaining the environment and bringing smart cities into existence. In order to achieve the objective of establishing smart cities and sustainability, currently Green IoT technology is essential to reduce the amount of carbon emissions and power consumption [21–23].

The increasing number of IoT devices leads to more energy consumption. Wake-up protocols and sleep schedules of IoT devices are typical example protocols that have been introduced for energy consumption and resource utilization [21]. Zhang et al. [23] provided techniques that can reduce energy consumption in IoT through efficient data transmission from various IoT-based devices, efficient energy management within data centres and designed energy-efficient policies. Similarly, Hu et al. [22] introduced Information and Communication Technology (ICT) that has

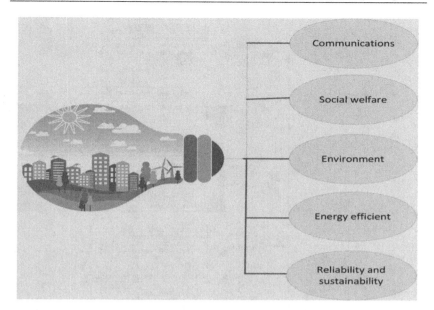

FIGURE 3.4 Aspects of Smart Cities

positive impact on the carbon emissions and energy consumption in the smart cities.

The existing literature on Green IoT-based smart cities is dispersed [25–26], which leads to inadequate recognition as well as importance to Green IoT. The current literature lacks the depth that can explain in detail the enabling techniques for IoT systems in smart cities improvising the QoS [27] and enabling ICT. The existing overall surveys are not comprehensively focused on the smart city strategies and techniques, which can facilitate green environment-based technology and devices.

Currently, the field of research and technology lacks a dedicated survey conducted on the various strategies and techniques to implement greener smart cities, via enabling ICT, reducing energy consumption, reducing CO_2 emissions, reducing waste management, improving sustainability and, making way for further studies to be performed in this field.

This study is more concentrated on the designing of energy-efficient policies, energy-efficient data centres, data transmission from IoT devices etc. This chapter focuses more on the survey of techniques and strategies, for enabling IoT to improve the eco-friendly and sustainability factors for smart cities. A few of the issues brought about by researchers post implementing

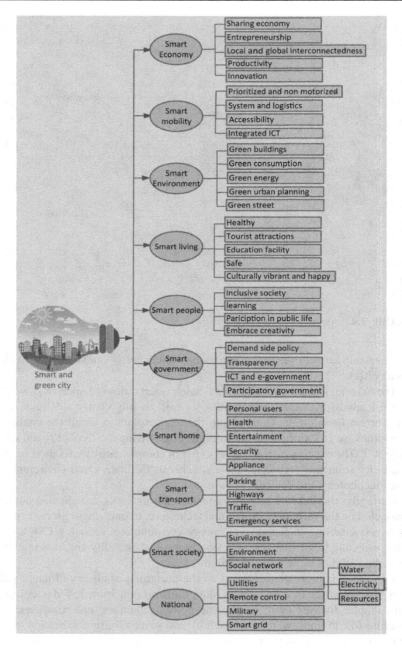

FIGURE 3.5   Smart City Applications

IoT are greenhouse gas emissions, energy usage etc. Huang et al. [24] introduced IoT for smart cities and addressed techniques in order to minimize energy consumption for Green IoT, and have further introduced the green ICT principle.

Some techniques have been further introduced for enabling Green IoT in order to facilitate energy efficiency. Arshad et al. [1] further discussed the concept of IoT applicable for smart cities, advantages, benefits and different applications.

The majority of research work focuses on factors like developing smart cities, strategies and techniques that have been developed based on collaborative IoT concepts, which can improve life quality, sustainability, eco-friendliness, citizen safety and the health of the environment.

A few of the research applications can be broadly categorized as follows:

1. IoT techniques to implement eco-friendly ICT aiming at reducing energy consumption and CO_2 emissions for designing a sustainable smart city.
2. Various strategies supporting energy-efficient techniques, reduced CO_2, reduced traffic and reduced resource usage in smart cities.
3. Designing waste management techniques to improve smart cities.
4. Advanced techniques used for smart city sustainability.
5. Surveying current ongoing research works and possible future techniques for smart cities' sustainability and energy efficiency, based on collaborative IoT.

3.5.1 ICT Technology Supporting Smart Cities

The ICT is the concept responsible for improving Green IoT technology in smart cities, making them more friendly and sustainable. ICT can reduce costs, resource consumption and pollution; interact with various city services; and enhance life quality. It may be quite difficult to design as well as to implement the concept of a smart city without ICT and its supporting applications.

ICT technologies reduce the overall climatic effect at the global level. With the help of ICT, applications grow becoming more energy efficient as a response to environmental awareness. The Green IoT concept is about hyper-technologies that make the IoT more conducible, thereby using facilities along with storage that needs subscribers to gather, store as well as access and manage different pieces of information [29]. The concept of green ICT supports operations such as gather, access, store and manage various data and information [24]. ICT plays a vital role in establishing the green component, which can provide benefits to society, i.e., saving energy that is required for designing, manufacturing and distributing ICT equipment and devices. Multiple research has been conducted over the green ICT technologies as referred to by Huang et al. [24] and Yogi and Bhavani [29]. Yogi and Bhavani [29] discussed using ICT applications and strategies to reduce CO_2 emissions and energy consumption.

ICT technologies play a vital role in reducing CO_2 emissions and energy consumption to Green IoT applications in smart cities, i.e., smart transportation, smart building, smart parking and so on [30].

An eco-friendly smart world can be achieved as a result of rapid development of science and technology, where the aim is towards making the world "Smart." As the world is moving towards being hi-tech, people can be automatically as well as collaboratively served via the smart devices, smart transportation, smart environments etc.

The concept of Green IoT devices is more apt into communicating towards the real world, proficiently focusing on saving energy and toxic waste [4]. Several application areas of Green IoT-based smart city (Figure 3.5) are as follows:

1. *Smart homes:* A Green IoT concept facilitates homes to be equipped with heating, lighting and electrical devices, which can be controlled and monitored remotely via smart devices such as smartphones or computers. The smart equipment designed for smart homes includes waste removal, ultrasonic showers, cots that make/change sheets themselves, lighting created artificially or non-natural sunrise, computer or smart device capable of making suggestions tailored as per users' choice, electric-insulated soundproof rooms and windows [1], soundproof energy grounds, hidden computers or smart devices, microphones, sensors and electronics devices/systems throughout the house and many more. A few of the high-technology items based on artificial intelligence include central computing systems or smart devices that can accept voice-based commands through voice sensor devices equipped with voice recognition technology, which can distinguish between occupants for adapted reactions with respect to its appropriate actions.

2. *Industrial automation:* The industry is currently revolutionizing itself towards automation implementing the concept of Industry 4.0 that allows fully computerized tasks with or without manual efforts. The industrial automation structure has been designed towards enabling a single industry operator into controlling the entire industries appliances.

3. *Smart health care:* IoT concept is into reforming healthcare industry post pandemic era by placing advanced technology-based sensors

that are connected with internet that are capable of producing real-time critical data [28]. It helps into accomplishing three major key effects of well-organized healthcare services focused on achievement in three major areas: better-quality access to care, enlarged care quality and reduced care costs.

4. *Smart grid:* The smart grid component is an electronic device offering the attractive feature of delivering energy at the lowermost cost level. The smart grid component maintains the balance providing efficiency, undergoing adjusting and re-adjusting for the optimal delivery of energy at the lowermost cost trying to achieve highest excellence possible. The smart grid technology has an overall effect, which aims at offering customers the skills to participate in the solution.

5. *Smart farming:* The smart farming concept is about farming supervision based on innovation designed to increase the number of agricultural items. Various agriculturists have used different novel approaches like global positioning systems (GPS), scanning of soil, data management systems and IoT innovations. Via correct estimation of factors such as variations within the field, adjusting the procedures as required, farmers can expand the adequacy of pesticides and manure and use them to specification [28]. Via smart farming methods, farmers may further use technology for screening requirements of individual seed types and changing their nutrition correspondingly, upgrading the overall farming process.

3.5.2 Smart Data Centres for Smart Cities

The data centres in the smart city technology play the role of data repository for efficient data management, data storage as well as the machine disseminating the gathered data that from smart city devices. The massive number of IoT-based devices requires uninterrupted internet connectivity while operating in the smart city.

The entire process of data management and transformation of raw data into information over a smart city is currently unimaginable without the presence of the data centre. The handling of heterogeneous kind and nature of data involves huge amounts of energy [22], high costs of operation and high CO_2 footprints while dealing with unique data from different applications consuming huge quantities of energy. The production of big data undergoes a constant rise as a result of various ubiquitous things, such as mobile devices, actuators, sensors, RFID etc. Huang et al. [24] and Atzori et al. [30] put forth several techniques for efficient power management such as renewable energy, utilizing efficient dynamic power management, designing more energy-efficient hardware, constructing efficient softwares, designing novel energy-efficient data centre architectures, using accurate data centre power models, drawing support from communication and computing techniques, improving air management, consolidating servers, finding optimal environment etc.

The refinement of the features of a data centre includes airflow and processing, looking for optimal environment, betterment of the air management and consolidation of server-related operations. Kawsar and Nakajima [31] proposed multiple techniques to improvise as well as predict energy efficiency of data centres and their various components. The literature survey conducted by Hydra Project [32] provided a method to reduce the power consumption, keeping intact the cooling efficiency feature of the data centres. Some futuristic research works have also explored the energy-efficient context-aware broker framework mechanisms with an aim to efficiently handle next-generation data centres [33]. The study conducted proposed a green data centre with an air-conditioning design feature based on cloud techniques, comprising two subsystems (i.e., air conditioning in the data centre system and cloud management platform) [34]. It included features like environmental monitoring, air conditioning, communication, temperature control and ventilation. On the other hand, a cloud platform provides services like data storage, up-layer application, big data analysis and prediction. The power consumption of the data centres can be reduced while maintaining QoS requirement via the Ant Colony System (ACS)-based VM [35–36] by achieving a near-optimal solution, where the VM reduces energy consumption while maintaining the desired QoS [37]. Figure 3.6 illustrates the required impacts for greening the data centre for smart cities.

Power consumption can be drastically reduced with the help of dynamic speed scaling techniques [38]. With respect to speed scaling techniques, various researchers have addressed signal processing [39], network devices [30–31] and parallel processors [36], which can probably save energy. Researchers from the Hydra Project [32] have proposed a hybrid model that combined sleep states by changing the speed during the processing of a task for energy reduction.

Sundmaeker et al. [35] conceptualized a centralized network power controller system designed based on data collected over the traffic. The statistic servers are formed, which collect data that are used for performing activities such as the aggregation of transportation and VM assignment, which in due course are used for migrating the target data centre. The literature survey conducted by the authors indicated that bandwidth and VM reduced the network power consumption for a given data centre topology. In order to optimize the power usage in data centre, networks with guaranteed connectivity and bandwidth utilization, researchers Zhang et al. [23] proposed two major methods: core level and pod level. The main purpose of the core level aims at core switches, whereas the pod level defines the aggregation switches.

Furthermore, the study in the article is focused on reducing energy by adopting two major steps:

i. Allocating VM to the server to minimize the traffic amount and
ii. Balancing traffic flows by reducing the number of active switches.

As stated in previous sections, the importance of availability and sustainability for future worth of data centres in smart cities requires features that support processing of huge quantities of data, categorized as big data collected over various sensors dispersed all over the city.

In order to enhance the technological infrastructure and cost reduction factor, the processing of big data requires communication networks, virtualization systems and storage access. Here, the smart data centres manage efficiently as well as effectively the smart cities, making themselves the core technology; providing advanced features such as increased access security and passive sensitometer; achieving balanced sustainability etc.; managing the overall city environment; providing sustainable development for city development; effectively and efficiently coordinating and controlling the resources required controlling energy from renewable resources; managing the mobility and traffic; measuring the emissions and pollutions; managing the growth of resources, i.e., air, water, light etc.; and leading other services such as recycling waste, public safety, health etc. Smart data centres are the major components of smart cities that will help create new technologies and architectures, which can support and manage smart cities for providing a better quality of life to the people. Figure 3.6. shows the overall impact achieved by making the smart Data Centers Green.

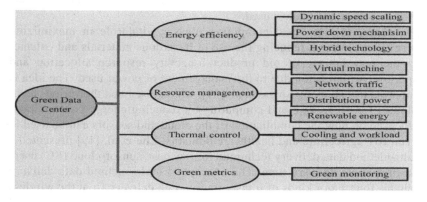

FIGURE 3.6 Required Impacts for Greening the Data Centre

3.5.3 Cloud Computing for Smart Cities

The concept of cloud computing may be considered essential as well as critical for building the smart cities' physical infrastructure. The physical enabling of the smart city concept needs both the combination of the decentralized cloud and the distributed open-source network. Hence, the huge quantities of diverse data is collected from various devices, which surround smart cities heavily dependent upon cloud computing services.

As we know, the smart city concept is about a high-quality lifestyle offered to people via advanced technology, management of natural resources, economic development etc. Hence, it is expected to intelligently provide the numerous facilities that could improve smart city applications, e.g., police transport, public safety, security, electric supply, water supply, internet connectivity and smart parking.

The concept of cloud computing is about providing unlimited computational service delivery via internet and unlimited storage. Here various heterogeneous devices (i.e., tablets, cameras, laptops and mobile phones) are connected through the cloud. The combination of cloud computing and IoT together provides good scope for researchers to further explore upon.

Cloud computing promotes eco-friendly products which can be reused as well as recycled. Zhou and Wang [18] proposed the green computing concept, highlighting the need of ICTs along with the trade-off between green computing and high-performance policies and expectations. Zhu et al. [19] proposed a green solution to IoT over a fog-supported network.

Hence, efficient cloud computing technology supports maximization of energy consumption, reduction of various hazardous materials as well as supporting the old products' recyclability. Moreover, they also aim to have achieved product longevity resource allocation and paperless virtualization due to the management of power used.

Further, efficient cloud computing plays a vital role in maximizing energy consumption, reducing the use of hazardous materials and enhancing the recyclability of old product longevity resource allocation and paperless virtualization due to the management of power used. The idea is supported in a study by Spiess et al. [37], which discussed the various technologies for greening cloud computing by reducing energy consumption. It focused on how the combination of the cloud and sensors can be used in Green IoT agriculture and healthcare domains. Zhu et al. [19] presented a multi-method data delivery technique for low cost, sensor-cloud (SC) users and immediate delivery time. The concept of multi-method data delivery includes four major kinds of transportation, i.e., delivery from the wireless sensor network to SC users, delivery from cloudlet to SC users, delivery from the cloud to SC users and delivery from SC users to SC users. The technology of green cloud computing mainly revolves around minimizing utility power [33]. Thus, Bleecker [33] introduced essential techniques that can improve the data centre's power performance. Private and public clouds require energy consumption in numerous operations like data processing, switching, transmission and storage [34].

Numerous researchers works till date have been conducted on green cloud computing [22, 31, 35–36], which provides promising solutions for reduced energy consumption, power-saving methods designed over VM and various energy-efficient resource allocation mechanisms with related tasks, with efficient methods for energy-saving systems. The Hydra Project [32] explored trade-offs over energy performance for consolidation, which offers desired workload distribution across various servers and saves energy. Bleecker [33] summarized the strategies that are used for economic use of resources and green cloud based on multi-tenancy, dynamic provisioning, server utilization and data centre efficiency.

The performance of cloud computing is compared by metrics like service rate, packet arrival rate and response time for the efficiency improvement over the power cost and server utilization [37]. However, a VM scheduling algorithm plays a vital role in greening cloud computing, which leads to energy consumption minimization [38–39]. In the case of Kostelnik et al. [38], a machine algorithm is used for migration of loads of hosts, dynamic voltage frequency scaling and shutdown of underutilized host features. The result of using algorithms led to improving power consumption. Cloud computing availability in smart cities could help ease big data storage, transforming over the real-time data processing as well as performing an analysis over real-time data.

Therefore, the concept of cloud computing improves metrics such as speed, sharpness as well as cost savings by providing network access on demand for sharing computing resources, which may be scaled as and when required and rapidly provisioned. The combination of IoT and cloud computing also contributes to healthcare applications such as disease identification and prediction intelligently in smart cities [10]. Ge et al. [11] presented an intelligent model for healthcare-related applications and services in smart cities, using concepts such as parallel particle swarm optimization and particle swarm optimization. The proposed models solve task scheduling, reduce medical requests execution time and maximize medical resources utilization and IoT. Some articles also use advanced research methodology such as Kawsar and Nakajima [31] proposed fog, cloud and IoT to mitigate processing loads and reduce cost and time.

3.5.4 Communication Networks for Smart Cities

The IoT technology can be made greener by the implementation of green wireless communication technology. The context of green communication impacts the performance in terms of sustainability, energy efficiency, energy awareness and making communication environmentally aware. The overall idea of a green communication network is all about low CO_2 emissions, low radiation exposure as well as low energy consumption. In their article, Ge et al. [13] proposed network planning based on genetic algorithm optimization, which claims to reduce significantly the CO_2 emit ion and gives low radiation exposure. The concept was driven forward by an article by Luo et al. [14], which improved the maximization of data rate, minimizing of CO_2 emissions in cognitive WSNs.

The study and analysis of energy efficiency in 5G have been designed on the basis of mobile communication networks and are put forth in three major categories, i.e., theory models, application and technology developments. Quite a number of researchers have addressed solar methods for saving energy and enhancing QoS [27, 39], as a reliable energy-saving methodology [13]. Moreover, the stochastic geometric approach is applied to achieving energy efficiency as well as fulfilling QoS maintenance requirements [14].

All the more, the utility-based adaptive duty cycle algorithm proposed by Ge et al. [11] is all about reducing delay, increasing energy efficiency and keeping a long lifetime [15]. However, the hypertext transfer protocol was applied to reduce delay and enhance the lifetime for providing reliability [16]. The development network's performance depends on the requirements based on decreasing energy usage, reducing the emission of CO_2 for providing a healthy environment and green cities.

The 5G network focuses on reducing energy utilization, which can bring about green communication and healthy environments. In 2020, the forecast of green communication is all about communication devices where the objects can communicate effectively and efficiently using smart and green techniques that can bring about a healthy and green life. 5G technology is essential for improving the reliability factor as well as improving QoS of communication between the machines and humans. 5G technology also supports huge large areas' connectivity, reduces latency, saves energy and provides higher data rate. Some 5G services for society include robotics communication, e-health, interaction, human and robotics, media, transport and logistics, e-learning, public safety, e-governance, automotive and industrial systems etc.

3.5.5 Wireless Sensor Networks for Smart Cities

The concept of WSN is a combination of sensors and wireless communication mode operating in coherence for many applications such as fire detection, object tracking, environmental monitoring, evolving constraints in the military [13], controlling machine health, monitoring industrial process and many more. WSNs represent the critical technology that has made IoT flourish. A sensor device combines quite a number of small, low-power as well as low-cost electronic devices. They consist of base stations, sinks and sensor nodes. The sensor node is made up of communication unit, sensing unit, processing unit and power unit that help it in measuring global as well as local environments such as pollution, weather, health care, agricultural fields etc. The sensors interact over wireless channels, delivering to the nearest base station's sensory data via ad hoc technology. Luo et al. and Koomey [15] introduced sleep mode, which could save sensor powers for an elongated stretch of time indirectly supporting Green IoT concept. A few more contributions are extensions or minor diversions of the existing concept, for example, Bilal et al. [16] proposed the nearest most used routing algorithm, where the nearest node actively participates in transmitting ion and receiving data, while the rest of the nodes are in sleep mode and continue sensing during the idle mode. The concept permits any node wanting to send data to any node and wakes up all the nodes with roots successively sending the data in accordance.

As the sending data finishes, the nodes are reset to sleep mode. Sensors absorb and use the energy harvested directly from the environment, e.g., the sun, kinetic energy and temperature differentials. The combination of WSN and energy-harvested technologies is crucial in green world. They are technically cost-effective with respect to energy harvesting with batteries' longevity. Many techniques enable sensor networks into Green IoT, e.g., sensing selection, energy overheads for context-aware sensing [15], sleep schedule planning to save energy, reducing the communication delay between sensors nodes etc. Here the battery power is considered the most critical resource in WSN influencing the network lifetime. Thus, the main goal here is to reduce energy consumption and contribute reliable/robust transmission without compromising the overall QoS [20].

The growth and development while incorporating sustainability solutions increase mobility, which improves the overall environmental impacts. Priyadumkol et al. [17] introduced the concept of smart mobility for autonomous vehicles and highlight the various smart city challenges. The benefits of mobility for enhancing smart city sustainability are put forth by Zhou and Wang [18], which aim at achieving increased people's safety, reduced noise pollution, improved transfer of speed, reduced traffic as well as reduced transferring costs. Furthermore, Zhu et al. [19] also discussed multiple ways in which information shared with IoT supports the sustainable value chain network.

3.5.6 Reducing Pollution Hazards in Smart Cities

Tracking and monitoring air pollution have been currently an important issue to deal with in our environment, life society etc. The smart sensors in smart cities are used to monitor the environmental pollution. Considering the transmission power of sensors for sending data in real time is limited; hence, they are carried by drones.

A few advanced technologies equipped with drones introduced solar-powered drones that carried CO_2 sensing integrated with a WSN. Under this, the drones provide remote autonomous food safety and quality. Similarly, Luo et al. [14] proposed drones that are equipped with off-the-shelf sensors that can track tasks. Some authors have suggested adopting a pollution-based drone control system. The overall experiences in applying drones have also been explained by Zhu et al. [19]. Huang et al. [20] provided an analysis of investigating water pollution in Southwest China affected by low air pressure, high altitude, severe weather, strong air turbulence and clouds as well as the prediction of carbon footprints in ICT sectors.

Although the concept of air pollution is a result of climate change, drone technology currently may be considered as a vital system capable of monitoring air pollution and contribute to improving the life quality in smart cities.

3.5.7 Waste Management in Smart Cities

Various smart cities moving towards development are becoming smarter as well as greener. Organizations, both in the public and private sectors, are looking for efficient solutions for maximizing the collection levels via intelligent techniques and smart devices, such as smart sensors, cloud platforms and IoT. Various researchers have proposed quite novel concepts such as intelligent waste collection, cyber-physical system for smart cities based on IoT sensing prototype etc. The IoT-based sensor prototype measures waste level within the trash can and bins and sends data to the cloud over the internet in order to store and process. Depending on the collected data, the optimization process can efficiently and dynamically maintain as well as manage the waste collection by intimating the workers for necessary action.

The authors try to improvise the strategies regarding waste collection efficiency over the real time through ensuring that when the trash bins were full, the workers would collect in real time, reducing the waste overflow. Thus, IoT enabled overall waste monitoring and management solutions within the smart cities through connected sensors integrated with the container.

IoT is considerably the new technology that can be used for waste management as well as provide an efficient solution in a variety of ways such as IoT software in waste management, cost efficiency, waste collection and reduced greenhouse gas emissions. Moreover, advanced technologies like artificial intelligence and IoT are making a huge contribution to reducing the cost and complexity of automated waste systems via improving efficiency, productivity and safety and minimizing environmental impacts. The disposed waste in any condition is a challenge due to health issues it can bring about.

3.5.8 Sustainability in Smart Cities

The concept of urban planning has become quite essential to survive within a developed sustainable and green smart city. Ensuring the health and the well-being of every citizen is quite a necessary factor for almost all countries in the world. The overall structure and design of sustainable green cities directly influence human health as well as well-being.

Through the concept of smart networking and environmentally friendly habitats, various ecological resources have been examined and maintained, where the environmental benefits provided are immense. The technology and its applications are merely not about making human life healthy but also growing healthy trees, wildlife and plants. The energy-efficient practices adopted can be said to be the key towards implementing the green sustainable city. The smart as well as green disposal techniques help into curtailing the probability of greenhouse gas emissions.

The concept of sustainable green cities has led to changes in both technical and social innovations. Sustainable and green cities concepts also include green spaces and smart agricultural resources. In order to keep the smart city green, some mandatory steps to be undertaken include renewal of resources, reduction of the ecological footprint, reduction of pollution etc. IoT plays a vital role in improving smart cities to become more liveable, resilient, green and sustainable. IoT and smart city technology are the mandatory needs for developing as well as establishing a smart society and improving life quality. A smart city is built over an intelligent framework that consists of complex ubiquitous networks, objects, government and connectivity for data transmission. The data collected over the cloud of smart cities for applications is managed and analysed appropriately and is used for decision making and transforming actions into real time, enhancing the way we work and live.

The Green IoT has a major role in smart cities aiming at making it all the greener as well as a sustainable place to work and live. The Green IoT technique and technologies provide an attractive output in big data analysis, making smart cities significantly safer, smarter and all the more sustainable. Zheng et al. [12] discussed the achievements of the big data towards improving the overall life quality by reducing pollution and utilizing resources in a more efficient manner. In order to manage resources used by IoT for attaining sustainable and green smart cities, Ge et al. [13] proposed concepts of delay tolerant streaming, hybrid adaptive bandwidth and power techniques during media transmission within a smart city. Furthermore, Luo et al. [14] discussed a sustainable Green IoT environment.

A smart sustainable city typically uses ICT techniques in order to make the life easy and comfortable via technology. The efficiency of modern technology and competitiveness try to meet present as well as future generations' economic, social and environmental needs. A sustainable smart city may be defined as an innovative city that makes use of ICT and IoT technologies, which could improve life quality, service quality and competitiveness. It also ensures meeting the needs of the present and future people regarding social, economic, cultural and environmental aspects.

With the majority of the crowd moving into urban and smart cities, the issues related to energy resource management, sustainability and sharing and utilities of emerging technologies require the majority of focus.

3.6 INTEGRATING RADIO FREQUENCY IDENTIFICATION AND SMART OBJECTS INTO A UNIFIED INTERNET OF THINGS ARCHITECTURE

As the literature suggests, since the last decade, IoT has been successful in attracting attention by portraying the vision of conceiving a global infrastructure consisting of networked physical objects, able to implement anytime, anyplace establishing the connectivity for anything. The concept of IoT is about a world where physical objects and humans along with virtual data, environments, etc., interact with each other within the same space and the given time.

The IoT concept was inspired by RFID development community, which referred to the possibility of discovering information regarding any tagged object through browsing the internet address or database entry corresponding to a particular RFID.

Many research activities have been initiated thereafter, which focused on linking tens of thousands of sensor networks through convergence of technologies, which grants permission to companies as well as individuals for

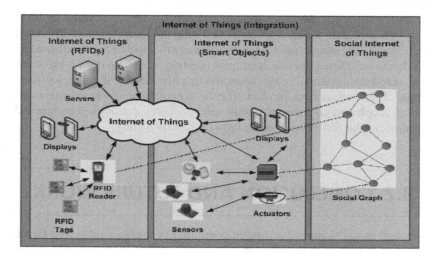

FIGURE 3.7   Integrated IoT High-Level Architecture

keeping track of each physical item on the earth. Similar studies highlighted the issue of developing an IoT architecture, limited with respect to global implementation due to the dichotomy imposed by RFID nature, i.e., the heterogeneity in nature between the plain and passive RFID tags and the networked RFID readers. A few researchers have taken up the issue and are working towards an alternative architectural model for the IoT, which may be loosely coupled or a decentralized system of smart objects—i.e., autonomous physical/digital objects add on with sensing, processing and networking capabilities.

The integration among various IoT architectures with respect to smart objects as shown in Figure 3.7 can be imposed by two facts:

1. RFID tags are implementable in almost all aspects of daily life, and moreover they are cheap, easily produced etc.
2. The research on nano-electronic devices and polymers electronics is used in order to develop cheap, nontoxic as well as disposable electronic sensors and objects.

The applications that are developed over an IoT architecture that are compromised by RFID tags are limited to identification and tracking. The integration of sensing and acting smart objects into passive RFID tags may enable the integration of quite a lot of new applications within the IoT context ranging from sensor and automation-specific applications to combined inter-domain applications. In the book, *Cluster of European Research Projects on IoT*, published in 2010, it was claimed that domains accelerated by the implementation of IoT-based applications. The authors mentioned that domains that will be highly affected by IoT datum include automotive, intelligent building, telecommunications, health care, aerospace, aviation, independent living, pharmaceutical, retail, logistics, supply chain management, product lifecycle management, environmental monitoring, people and good transportation, safety, security, privacy, agriculture and breeding, media and entertainment, insurance and recycling.

3.7 CONCLUSION AND FUTURE WORK

The chapter has discussed advanced computing techniques related to Green IoT in detail. It includes various advanced technical concepts like smart objects, edge computing, green data centres, cloud computing and how the green factor can be integrated into it to make it all the more pro-environment. The chapter discusses in detail the futuristic smart city and how the green and environmentally friendly smart device components playing an integrated part of it are able to strike the balance between achieving a good quality of life in an eco-friendly manner preserving the natural resources to the most. The chapter finally discusses the RFID factor and smart objects integrated in the IoT architecture layout, which can help in tracking objects from anywhere, anyplace, in real-time mode. This concept opens the door for future advancements of putting all the smart objects and devices integrated with RFID in a single canvas for easy monitoring and control in a more centralized manner.

REFERENCES

[1] R. Arshad, et al. "Green IoT: An Investigation on Energy Saving Practices for 2020 and Beyond," *IEEE Access*, vol. 5, pp. 15667–15681, 2017.

[2] M. Chiang, T. Zhang. "Fog and IoT: An Overview of Research Opportunities," *IEEE Internet of Things Journal*, vol. 3, no. 6, pp. 854–864, 2016.

[3] G. Bedi, et al. "Review of Internet of Things (IoT) in Electric Power and Energy Systems," *IEEE Internet of Things Journal*, vol. 5, no. 2, pp. 847–870, 2018.

[4] M.A.M. Albreem, et al. "Green Internet of Things (IoT): An Overview," *2017 IEEE 4th International Conference on Smart Instrumentation, Measurement and Application (ICSIMA), IEEE*, 28–30 November 2017, Putrajaya, Malaysia.

[5] V. Tahiliani, M. Dizalwar, "Green IoT Systems: An Energy Efficient Perspective," *2018 Eleventh International Conference on Contemporary Computing (IC3)*, IEEE, Noida, India, 2018. DOI: 10.1109/IC3.2018.8530550.

[6] Z. Ning, et al. "Green and Sustainable Cloud of Things: Enabling Collaborative Edge Computing," *IEEE Communications Magazine*, vol. 57, no. 1, pp. 72–78, 2018.

[7] M. Guo, L. Li, Q. Guan, "Energy-Efficient and Delay-Guaranteed Workload Allocation in IoT-Edge-Cloud Computing Systems," *IEEE Access*, vol. 7, pp. 78685–78697, 2019.

[8] F. Tao, et al. "CCIoT-CMfg: Cloud Computing and Internet of Things-Based Cloud Manufacturing Service System," *IEEE Transactions on Industrial Informatics*, vol. 10, no. 2, pp. 1435–1442, 2014.

[9] M. Chen, S. Mao, Y. Liu, "Big Data: A Survey," *Mobile Networks and Applications*, vol. 19, no. 2, pp. 171–209, 2014.

[10] H.-P. Chiang, C.-F. Lai, Y.-M. Huang, "A Green Cloud-Assisted Health Monitoring Service on Wireless Body Area Networks," *Information Sciences*, vol. 284, pp. 118–129, 2014.

[11] X. Ge, H. Cheng, M. Guizani, T. Han, "5G Wireless Backhaul Networks: Challenges and Research advances," *Network, IEEE*, vol. 28, no. 6, pp. 6–11, 2014.

[12] K. Zheng, X. Zhang, Q. Zheng, W. Xiang, and L. Hanzo, "Quality-of-Experience Assessment and Its Application to Video Services in LTE Networks," *Wireless Communications, IEEE*, vol. 22, no. 1, pp. 70–78, 2015.

[13] X. Ge, X. Huang, Y. Wang, M. Chen, Q. Li, T. Han, C.-X. Wang, "Energy-Efficiency Optimization for MIMO-OFDM Mobile Multimedia Communication Systems with QoS Constraints," *Vehicular Technology, IEEE Transactions*, vol. 63, no. 5, pp. 2127–2138, 2014.

[14] J. Luo, L. Rao, X. Liu, "Temporal Load Balancing with Service Delay Guarantees for Data Center Energy Cost Optimization," *Parallel and Distributed Systems, IEEE Transactions*, vol. 25, no. 3, pp. 775–784, 2014.

[15] J. Koomey, "Growth in Data Center Electricity Use 2005 to 2010," A Report by Analytical Press, Completed at the Request of the *New York Times*, p. 9, 2011.

[16] K. Bilal, S.U.R. Malik, O. Khalid, A. Hameed, E. Alvarez, V. Wijaysekara, R. Irfan, S. Shrestha, D. Dwivedy, M. Ali et al., "A Taxonomy and Survey on Green Data Center Networks," *Future Generation Computer Systems*, vol. 36, pp. 189–208, 2014.

[17] J. Priyadumkol, C. Kittichaikarn, "Application of the Combined Airconditioning Systems for Energy Conservation in Data Center," *Energy and Buildings*, vol. 68, pp. 580–586, 2014.

[18] L. Zhou, H. Wang, "Toward Blind Scheduling in Mobile Media. *IEEE Transactions on Multimedia*, vol. 15, no. 4, pp. 735–746, June 2013."

[19] C. Zhu, et al. "Green Internet of Things for the Smart World," *IEEE*, vol. 3, pp. 2151–2162, 2015.

[20] J. Huang., et al. "A Novel Deployment Scheme for the Green Internet of Things," *IEEE Internet of Things Journal*, vol. 1, no. 2, pp. 196–205, 2014.

[21] F.K. Shaikh, S. Zeadally, E. Exposito. "Enabling Technologies for Green Internet of Things," *IEEE Systems Journal*, vol. 11, no. 2, pp. 983–994, 2015.

[22] J. Hu, et al. "Graphene-Grid Deployment in Energy Harvesting Cooperative Wireless Sensor Networks for Green IoT," *IEEE Transactions on Industrial Informatics*, vol. 15, no. 3, pp. 1820–1829, 2018.

[23] D. Zhang, et al. "Two Time-Scale Resource Management for Green Internet of Things Networks," *IEEE Internet of Things Journal*, vol. 6, no. 1, pp. 545–556, 2018.

[24] H. Huang, et al. "Green Data-Collection from Geo-Distributed IoT Networks through Low-Earth-Orbit Satellites," *IEEE Transactions on Green Communications and Networking*, vol. 3, no. 3, pp. 806–816, 2019.

[25] R.K. Lenka, A.K. Rath, S. Sharma, "Building Reliable Routing Infrastructure for Green IoT Network," *IEEE Access*, vol. 7, pp. 129892–129909, 2019.

[26] S.F. Abedin, et al. "A System Model for Energy Efficient Green-IoT Network," *Event 2015 International Conference on Information Networking, ICOIN 2015* – Siem Reap, Cambodia, 2015.

[27] Jin, J., Gubbi, J., Luo, T., & Palaniswami, M. (2012, October). Network architecture and QoS issues in the internet of things for a smart city. In *2012 International Symposium on Communications and Information Technologies* (ISCIT) (pp. 956–961). IEEE.

[28] C.S. Nandyala, H.-K. Kim, "Green IoT Agriculture and Healthcare Application (GAHA)," *International Journal of Smart Home*, vol. 10, no. 4, pp. 289–300, 2016.

[29] M.K. Yogi., K.G.D. Bhavani, "Green IOT: Principles, Current Trends, Future Directions," *International Journal*, vol. 6, no. 3, pp. 156–158, 2018.

[30] L. Atzori, A. Iera, G. Morabito, "The Internet of Things: A Survey," *Computer Networks*, vol. 54, no. 15, pp. 2787–2805, 2010.

[31] F. Kawsar, T. Nakajima, "A Document Centric E. A. Kosmatos et al. Copyright © 2011 SciRes. AIT 12 Framework for Building Distributed Smart Object Systems," *2009 IEEE International Symposium on Object/Component/Service-Oriented Real-Time Distributed Computing*, Tokyo, 17–20 March 2009, pp. 71–79.

[32] Hydra Project, 2010. http://www.hydramiddleware.eu.

[33] J. Bleecker, "A Manifesto for Networked Objects—Cohabiting with Pigeons, Arphids, and Aibos in the Internet of Things," blog, 2006.

[34] "Pigeons That Blogs," Project, 2010. http://www.beatrizdacosta.net/pigeonblog. php.

[35] H. Sundmaeker, P. Guillemin, P. Friess, S. Woelffle, "Vision and Challenges for Realising the Internet of Things," *Cluster of European Research Projects on the Internet of Things,* Brussels, Europe, European Commission, 2010.

[36] S.D. Deugd, R. Carroll, K. Kelly, B. Millett, J. Ricker, "SODA: Service Oriented Device Architecture," *IEEE Pervasive Computing*, Vol. 5, No. 3, pp. 94–96, 2006. doi:10.1109/MPRV.2006.59.

[37] P. Spiess, et al., "SOA-Based Integration of the Internet of Things in Enterprise Services," *IEEE Proceedings of International Conference on Web Services*, Los Angeles, 6–10 July 2009, pp. 968–975.

[38] P. Kostelnik, M. Sarnovsky, J. Hreno, M. Ahlsen, P. Rosengren, P. Kool, M. Axling, "Semantic Devices for Ambien Environment Middleware," *The Internet of Things and Services, 1st International Research Workshop*, Sophia-Antipolis, 18–19 September 2008.

[39] P. Hitzler, M. Krötzsch, B. Parsia, P.F. Patel-Schneider, S. Rudolph, "OWL 2 Web Ontology Language: Primer," 2009. http://www.w3.org/TR/owl2-primer/

Energy-Efficient Design towards Green Internet of Things

4

4.1 INTRODUCTION

The concept of green computing encompasses various concepts and schemes offered as well as encouraged by governments such as Carbon Reduction Commitment (CRC) schemes, the Climate Change Agreement (CCA) or the European Union Emission Trading Scheme (EU ETS), which support as well as mandate companies to revaluate their IT resources usage.

The term "energy conservation" is a frequently used word that is being used quite frequently these days by both industry and academia. To appreciate as well as understand what real energy conservation techniques are, it is necessary to understand the theory of conservation working as its backbone architecture.

4.1.1 Understanding Energy Conservation

The concept of energy conservation is the method of reducing demand over a limited supply and support the rebuild of the supply for the concerned product. Quite a promising method of doing the same is replacement of used energy with an alternate source.

With respect to fossil fuels, conservation of energy includes identifying new ways for digging into the earth's supply so that publicly used oil fields do not get drained out. There are various methods that allow the fields to replenish

DOI: 10.1201/9781003204503-4

FIGURE 4.1   Energy Conservation Models Used in Smart Factories [1]

themselves with more fuel, which requires time and efforts since the aim is to alleviate excess demand over the supply in hundreds of years' time to allow nature to recover.

It is a universally accepted truth that conservation of energy is conserving money that is all the more facilitated by integration of the concept of IoT with the electrical devices that consume energy making the system overall smart.

Quite a number of innovative devices have been developed based on low energy consumption. Some examples are the use of motion-sensitive bulbs, limited time use of air conditioners, cutting the number of shifts and functioning hours etc. Adding the concept of Internet of Things (IoT) enables direct energy savings for the various smart factories of today producing a variety of smart appliances.

Multiple hybrid models have been recommended by experts with IoT-based real-time monitoring systems in order to ensure optimized use of energy, but such systems merely assist in tracking energy consumption rather than directly leading to energy conservation as shown in Figure 4.1. The real-time energy monitoring system generally supports better predictions of energy usage as well as becomes a guide to implementing the right load level for energy-consuming devices [1].

Energy conservation techniques: Energy consumption and conservation are currently challenges faced by the majority of industries as well as on the domestic front. With the advent of new technology and a variety of electric devices being launched in the market, the prediction of energy consumed surpasses the amount of energy produced, making it mandatory to devise smart home energy management system-based devices as well as energy conservation techniques to be adopted as a mode of saving energy. A few examples of energy conservation methods are as follows:

a. *Electrical energy billing:* The electrical energy billing process is categorized as having two components: demand charge and run-time/consumption-related charges. Demand load can typically be the peak load provided by the electricity service providers during the power grid. It has fixed limit, crossing which incurred prompt penalties of 20 times higher than the usual rates.

Avoiding measures includes reducing the total load needed by the machinery or ensuring that the threshold limit is seldom reached.

b. *The problem with motors:* The machinery being used in various industries such as electrical motors and HVAC systems consume heavy quantities of electricity. A motor can be said to be under-loaded, while it's in the range where efficiency falls remarkably with the decrease of load. Most electric motors have been in-built designed to run at 50% to 100% of rated load. The maximum efficiency of machines is typically near 75%. A drop of load below the 50% rated load tends to lower the efficiency dramatically.

In the majority of cases, some operating motors are either overloaded, resulting in overheating, or underloaded, performing at 40% of their capacity, resulting in huge spikes with respect to energy consumption. The oversized motors incur high initial cost and are quite expensive to repair and maintain. The undersized motors do not perform well and end up causing higher losses than properly sized electric motors. This calls for attention of researchers to design smart and flexible motors, which can adjust according to the load capacity dynamically in real-time mode.

c. *Addressing a wide range of energy consumers:* Apart from regular electrical consumption of motors and HVAC, IoT can also deal with various energy sources and resources that include:

1. Air compressors—i.e., the source of air across plants.
2. Boilers that are used as source of steam across plants.
3. Backup generators serving as an alternative electricity source during the failure of primary source of fuels, which includes diesel, coal, wood, solar and batteries used to run above systems.

4.2 ENERGY OPTIMIZATION TECHNIQUES

In the field of networking, the energy is consumed for almost multiple essential tasks such as sensing, communicating, processing and actuating within and across the network layers. Various architectural elements that participate in the network-related activity communicate with each other increasing the overall energy consumption. The various principles and model designed to optimize energy consumption are based on some or the other divergent network-related devices.

4.3 SYSTEM MODEL FOR ENERGY-EFFICIENT GREEN INTERNET OF THINGS NETWORK

The layered architecture of an IoT network mainly focuses on achieving factors like pervasiveness and ubiquity in various IoT systems via sensing, analysing, communicating and processing of huge quantities of data [2]. It is a combination of both the hardware and software technologies, communication protocols and processing technologies. The architecture under operation varies mainly as understated criteria:

a. Domain and design
b. QoS factors
c. Interoperability among network and many other essential factors

The network design also stresses upon the major power-hungry nodes, protocols, middleware elements and applications. The network architecture is divided into five major layers: Perception, Transport, Processing, Network and Application layers.

The components associated with each layer are shown in Figure 4.2.

The elements of the network architecture can be segregated into power-hungry and non-power-hungry components.

a. *Perception layer:* The perception layer senses various data and provides scheduling and communication with other sensors. The various important tasks associated with the layers are self-organized in nature capable of sensing and load balancing. The various elements

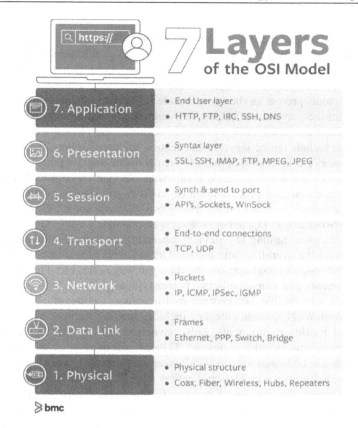

FIGURE 4.2   Components of the Network Layer

of this layer include sensors, radio frequency identification (RFID), sink nodes, actuators, gateway nodes and software solutions of which sink nodes, gateway nodes, actuators and passive RFID are categorized as power hungry [2–3]. The examples of applications of sensors are medical, military, chemical, ADC accelerometer, camera, GPS etc. [4].

b. *Transport layer:* This layer plays the role of transferring data from perception to the processing layer within a pipeline. The major components of this layer are 3G, LAN, Bluetooth, RFID, NFC, Wi-Fi, etc., of which typically the power-hungry components are NFC, Wi-Fi, coordinators, trust centre gateway, master-slave Bluetooth model etc. [1]. Examples of transport layer components are tags, reader, electrometer, short-range communication protocols, trust centre, gateway etc. [4].

c. *Processing/Middleware layer:* The processing layer is responsible for activities related to processing, storing and analysing huge quantities of data. The layer offers services such as allocating appropriate resources for efficient storage in virtual and physical machines, converting data into various required forms etc. The participating elements present in the layer include middleware databases, virtual machines, resource allocator, data centres, analytic centres and information convertor. A few examples of processing elements deployed also include online servers, data centres, microcontrollers, microprocessors etc. Examples of middleware databases that can potentially be utilized are semantic-based middleware, service-based middleware, event-based and process-oriented middleware, databases and data warehouses such as Contiki, Tiny-OS, RTOS, allocator CPU etc.

d. *Network layer:* The network layer is responsible for providing communication among the devices operating at various other layers within the overall system model. The elements of this layer include WSN nodes, cloud servers, big data gateway nodes etc. The device elements that consume heavy power typically are the WSN nodes, base stations, big data centres, routing gateway nodes etc. The low-power WSN element category includes sensing, computing, power and routing components, hubs, switches, IoT cellular operators, remote transmitting nodes etc. Typical examples of cloud servers that can be beneficial are WebBroker and virtual devices [5,6].

e. *Application layer:* The application layer is an abstract layer that facilitates the availing of services for the lower layers [7]. It offers the visualization of processed data in form of intelligent tasks. The examples of applications typically include the smart homes, smart buildings, smart vehicles, health care, smart environment, supply chain management, energy conservation etc., of which control systems are the power-consuming devices.

4.4 ENERGY-EFFICIENT DEVICES

Currently, the domestic use of electronic IoT devices is one of the major contributors to emitting harmful greenhouse gases as well as consuming a huge amount of energy. This indicates a need for using energy-efficient tools and strategies for reducing the emissions of carbon footprints.

At the home front, use of energy-efficient appliances reduces the electricity bills, protects the environment and enhances the quality of lifestyle. Thus, the more energy-efficient home appliances we use, the low is the electricity consumption as well as more protected the environment is from harmful gases such as carbon dioxide etc.

4.4.1 Green Machine-to-Machine Devices

The machine-to-machine (M2M) nodes that are logically connected to monitor data are embedded into M2M domain. With regard to the green M2M, the massive machines involved in M2M communications consume huge amounts of energy, specifically in the M2M domain [7]. In order to increase the energy efficiency of the devices, the following techniques can be employed:

1. Adjusting the transmission power to the level of bare minimal requirement.
2. Designing efficient communication protocols, e.g., routing protocols with the application of algorithmic and distributed computing techniques.
3. Designing and implementing joint energy-saving mechanisms like overload protection and resources allocation.
4. Employing energy-harvesting techniques, like spectrum sensing, spectrum management, interference mitigation, power optimization of Cognitive Radio (CR) etc. [2].

4.4.2 Green Direct Current

The direct current (DC) form of power used for handling data and applications consumes significant amounts of energy credited with high operational costs as well as emitting huge CO_2. In addition to the rise in data quantity generated by multiple things or objects that are pervasive and ubiquitous in nature like sensors, mobile phones etc. even more energy is needed. With the rise of smart technology-based devices, the energy efficiency for DCs has become quite significant [3]. For implementation of green DC, a few possible techniques that can be used to improve energy efficiency are:

• Use of renewable or green sources of energy like wind, solar power, water, heat pumps etc.
• Employing efficient and dynamic power-management techniques such as Turbo Boost, vSphere etc.

- Designing energy-efficient hardware designed by exploiting the features in Dynamic Voltage and Frequency Scaling (DVFS) techniques or vary-on/vary-off (VOVO) techniques [8].
- Designing and building data centres based on novel energy-efficient architecture such as Nano Data Centres (NDC) that can achieve power conservation.

4.4.3 Green Cloud Computing

In the cloud computing concept, the resources are often considered as cloud-based services, which are Infrastructure as a Service (IaaS), Platform as a Service (PaaS) and Software as a Service (SaaS). With the majority of applications moving onto the cloud, there is a huge demand of putting more cloud-based resources and infrastructure together, which ends up increasing power consumption, resulting in increased environmental issues and CO_2 emissions. This issue of increase in demand of power consumption calls for the need of designing devices that requires low energy consumption as well as builds efficient software that needs less energy as well as utilizes minimal hardware resources. Some applicable examples are power-saving virtual machine (VM) techniques like VM consolidation, VM placement and VM migration, of which the VM allocation has power-saving technologies [9] that can be applied. There are many other energy-efficient resource allocation mechanisms, which can be efficiently employed in the cloud platform, e.g., gossip-based resource allocation, auction-based resource allocation and related task scheduling mechanisms [10].

4.4.4 Reliability in Internet of Things Communication

In order to design and implement Green IoT concept, the major challenge currently faced by IoT is reliability, considering the fact that seldom sensor nodes are concurrently active in an IoT domain. The reliability factor in IoT communications can be improved by exploiting redundancy technologies such as information redundancy, temporal redundancy and spatial redundancy, which may be considered as efficient approaches. In the physical world of IoT communications, reliability is considered as one of the mandatory features within the network during system architecture, system development and sensor gateway communication within the network devices. Within the network, the information must be passed to receiver in a reliable manner at a low latency rate [11].

4.4.5 Energy Efficiency in Internet of Things Communication

Achieving energy efficiency in areas pertaining to sensors-based network is quite a challenging issue. The increase in regular consumption in the case of IoT-based communications is wisely dealt with by transmission adjustment to the power at the minimal required level, applying distributed computing and algorithms at appropriate places in order to design efficient communication protocols etc. The main focus here is to improvise the activity scheduling in order to effectively reduce energy consumption in IoT communications. This can be achieved by switching certain nodes to low-power operation or sleeping mode where only part of the nodes within the network remain active while operations related to the original network are preserved.

4.4.6 Green Design-Based Advanced Technologies

The current design trend for technology focuses on energy-efficient devices, network architectures, interconnections where researchers are working towards proposing communication protocols to cater to such smart and efficient devices. These leveraged technologies mostly focus on cutting down carbon emissions and enhancing energy efficiency through different energy optimization strategies. The advent of green ICT technologies and green IoT system has become quite popular due to its improved features such as efficiency, low energy consumption, reduced hazardous emissions, resources consumption and pollution. A few of the improved areas that can be considered for future improvisations are as follows:

1. *Internet of things:* The concept of IoT is one of the most on-demand technologies, which is showing a rapid growth almost in every part and field of the world. With a variety of new devices being added to the IoT network, diverse data being collected from various devices (often wirelessly), streaming down to edge devices and finally relayed to the cloud for further processing, IoT technology is able

to connect through different scales of architecture putting them into a single canvas. Researchers have predicted that in next few years, IoT devices may seem to consume almost 20% of global energy in the case of energy optimization. This opens the area for further research into designing energy-efficient IoT devices that require low energy.

2. *Lifetime of IoT devices:* The overall energy consumed by every device or node participating in the IoT network also limits the overall lifetime of the device as well as operation of network with dying out of devices used in hard-to-reach locations. In order to maintain the disrupted network services, it is essential to integrate the smart factor within the device in order to prolong the service intervals.

3. *Device architecture:* One of the research areas regarding smart devices development can be pertaining to undertake architectural decisions, which is technically performed during the concept development phase. It does not consider the power consumption factor into account as a design parameter covering the static, dynamic or integral energy demand, depending on the specific usage scenario, which opens the field for further exploration by domain experts [12].

4. *Classification of IoT-based devices:* The current design of the IoT-based devices lacks striking a balance between power-hungry transmission modules and regular node devices or modules where nodes can perform activities ranging from uploading extensive raw data and energy-intensive compression of data prior to sending to simple operation like local aggregation of sensor data and extraction of interesting features in order to reduce the volume of transmitted data. The classification of such device categories would help in designing smart energy management techniques that could channelize the amount of energy required for performing specific operations in the system.

5. *Transmission protocol:* Choice of transmission protocol in networks of many IoT nodes based on the required data rates and operating ranges is a crucial factor contributing towards the longevity of the network. A variety of protocols have been designed in order to carry out specific natures of transmission. For example, Zigbee and Bluetooth consuming low energy (BLE) can be used for special IoT protocols like Long Range, e.g., LoRa, Narrow Band IoT (NB-IoT) or even 5G variants can be used where heavy computation is involved.

6. *IoT components and algorithms:* The varying range and features of IoT components and algorithms have made design task enormous as

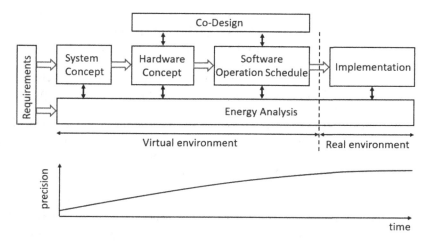

FIGURE 4.3   Various Techniques to Convert IoT into Green IoT

well as challenging. With an increase in automation, finding optimal solutions within the constraints to achieve the level of performance and energy conservation is all the more difficult to design and implement with the conceptual and developmental factors involved in the process as shown in Figure 4.3.

4.5 GREEN DESIGN

Murugesan [13] defined the concept of Green IoT as "the study and practice of designing, using, manufacturing, and disposing of servers, computers, and associated subsystems such as monitors, storage devices, printers, and communication network systems efficiently and effectively with minimal or no impact on the environment." Technically, Green IoT has three major concepts: design technologies, leverage technologies and enabling technologies.

The concept of Green IoT is to preserve natural resources, reducing the impact of technology on the environment and human health along with lowering the overall cost. Hence, Green IoT focuses on concepts like green manufacturing, green utilization, green design and green disposal [14].

1. *Green use:* The concept of green use is all about reducing energy consumed by devices such as computers and other information systems. The concept also touches upon sensitive topics like using these devices in an environmentally sound manner.
2. *Green disposal:* The concept of green disposal is regarding refurbishing and reusing old computers and recycling unwanted computers and other electronic equipment.
3. *Green design:* The green design is about designing energy-efficient technology as well as devices for implementing Green IoT, using highlighted techniques discussed in the previous section as well as using sound components, computers and servers with cooling equipment.
4. *Green manufacturing:* The concept of green manufacturing includes production of electronic components and computer devices and other associated subsystems with low to no impact on the environment.

4.6 VARIOUS TECHNIQUES TO CONVERT INTERNET O THINGS INTO GREEN INTERNET OF THINGS

Greening ICT deals with the technique of enabling technologies for Green IoT, which includes green RFID, green wireless sensor networks (GWSNs), green machine to machine (GM2M), green cloud computing (GCC), green data centres (GDCs) [8], green internet and green communication networks as shown in Figure 4.4. Greening the various components of ICT technologies plays a major role in achieving the concept of Green IoT while providing multiple benefits to the society such as reduced energy usage for designing, manufacturing and distributing ICT devices and equipment.

The concept of Green IoT is the practice of manufacturing, designing and disposing of computers, servers and associated hardware like printers, monitors, communicating equipment and storage devices efficiently with reduced effect on society and the environment [8]. Moving into greening the IoT, means looking for new resources, minimizing IoT's negative impact on human health and preserving the environment. The primary objective of greening IoT is towards reduction of CO_2 emissions and pollution, exploiting environmental conservation and minimizing the costs of

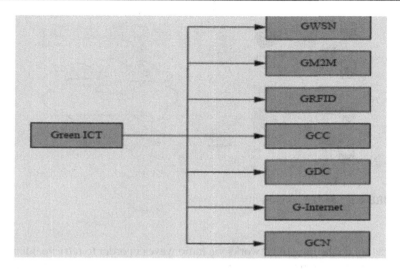

FIGURE 4.4 Green ICT Technologies

operating devices and the overall power consumption [12–15]. Aazam et al. [16] analysed and provided the details about industrial emissions, its impact on the environment etc. With the development of technique for greening the ICT technologies, the Green IoT concept shows high potential in supporting economic growth along with environmental sustainability [17]. The hot and emerging technologies that make the world greener and smarter are discussed as follows.

4.7 GREEN RADIO FREQUENCY IDENTIFICATION TECHNOLOGY

The concept of RFID is technically expressed as the combination of RF and ID, where RF is about the wireless communication technology and ID indicates the tag identification and information. The RFID technology has proved itself as quite a promising wireless communication system for being used in enabling the IoT system. The technology is capable to map the real world into the visual world even in the absence of any line of sight [18]. RFID may also carry on the task of data collection in an automated manner, as well as enabling

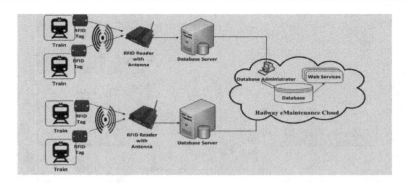

FIGURE 4.5　RFID Components

objects for connecting to networks via radio waves in order to retrieve, identify and store data in remote. The technology uses electromagnetic radio frequency barcodes to track objects in the store that has RFID incorporation products or items. The chief aim of using RFID in IoT is focused on storage of data and information streaming in via different channels.

The RFID-enabled devices may be classified into two categories: passive and active [18]. The passive things are not supported via batteries on the board, with use of minimal transmission frequency, whereas an active RFID device needs batteries that power the transmission signal.

The concept of green RFID opens up the option for moving the world towards green environment. It aims at improving the areas where emissions of the vehicle can possibly be reduced, and energy saving as well as improving the waste disposal methodology can be worked upon efficiently etc. Amin et al. [19] proposed a solution of incorporating green RFID antennas into embedded sensors.

The various RFID components are tags (for carrying identification data), reader (reading/writing tag data and interfaces with a system), antenna and station (process the data) as shown in Figure 4.5.

The use of RFID has a positive effect on organizational agility, which may have both direct and positive impacts on logistics and operational performance [20]. Qing et al. [21] focussed on raising the total lifetime of unmanned aerial vehicle (UAV) battery and RFID reader detection range.

The business groups typically perform combinations of UAV and RFID in order to support additional information, which can be implemented in a supply chain fashion of the management systems. A few researchers include multi-purpose RFID tags using UAV designed for environmental monitoring

[22]. Choi et al. [23] performed a comprehensive survey on UAV indoor localization techniques using passive Ultra High Frequency (UHF) far-field RFID systems, UAV localization and tracking for achieving simplicity and cost efficiency etc.

Some of their observations highlighted opening way towards potential research work for green RFID are:

a. Reducing the sizes of RFID tags making it reusable.
b. Energy-efficient techniques and protocols to be designed in order to avoid tag collision, tag estimation, overheating avoidance, adjusting transmission power level dynamically etc.

The concept of UAV is used for the purpose of data collection via RFID-based sensors. UAV and RFID sensors have been combined to work in accordance making together an overall powerful monitoring instrument. Here monitoring is typically required for a large area/harsh environment.

Many applications for RFID have been identified in areas related to transportation, production tracking, shipping, receiving, inventory control, regulatory compliance returns and recall management. Furthermore, RFID advantages include standardized, scalable approach, reliability and cost-effectiveness.

4.8 GREEN WIRELESS SENSOR NETWORK TECHNOLOGY

As we know, the vitality of sensors in IoT is typically built from small, low-power and low-cost electronic devices [24] that make the IoT system successful. The wireless communication and sensing mechanisms have led to wireless sensor networks (WSNs), which are composed of a large number of sensors and base station (BS) nodes etc. The sensor nodes here operate as sensing, processing and communicating units [24]. The sensor nodes are employed around the world, in various applications, measuring local and global environmental conditions such as weather, pollution, agricultural fields etc.

The idea of Green IoT is supported in articles [18–21], which arise for keeping sensor nodes in sleep mode for most of their life to save energy as shown in Figure 4.6.

Technically, the overall data communication takes place at ultra-low power enabling the sensors to employ natural sources of energy received

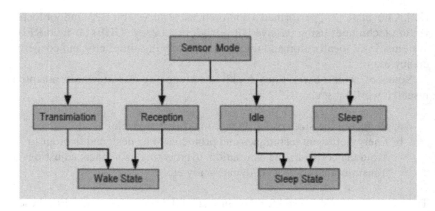

FIGURE 4.6   Various States of Sensor Modes

from the environment such as the sun, vibrations, kinetic energy, temperature differentials etc. [22].

As the WSN technology is responsible for transmission of signals efficiently along with allowing nodes to switch over to sleep mode in order to realize minimal power requirement, microprocessors in sensors are required to wake and sleep smartly [26]. The recent microprocessor trends and designs for WSNs include lowering energy consumption while increasing the processor speed. The green WSN is an emerging concept where the life span and throughput are optimized to the maximum level, while the CO_2 emissions are under consideration to be made greener, i.e., supplying adequate energy that can enhance the system lifetime while contributing reliable/robust transmission keeping intact the overall Quality of Service (QoS). Yaacoub et al. [27] have further investigated the concept of cooperative approach, which optimized the energy usage for greening WSNs. The overall idea of green WSN supports the concept of Green IoT [27], focuses on improving energy efficiency, network lifetime and reduced relay of nodes and reduction in the overall system budget. The work has been categorized to be implemented in four basic steps discussed as follows:

a. The creation of hierarchical system frameworks,
b. placement of sensor/actuator nodes,
c. clustering the nodes, creation of optimization models to build and established Green IoT,

d. calculation of minimal energy among the nodes. The experiments and analysis have proved that proposed Green IoT approach is energy-saving and cost-effective as compared to existing WSN deployment schemes. Therefore, it was concluded to be well suited for the Green IoT.

e. The integrated and distributed clustering mechanism employed in real-world applications has been elaborated by Oteafy et al. [17]. The integration techniques seem to improve the lifetime of the sensor nodes in environment-based applications. As we know sensors play an important role in environmental monitoring and greenhouse control [28]. Hence, the green designation with sensors may be considered as suitable for monitoring and risk identification purpose. Some of the contributions of these kinds of models are:

a. Periodic data collection and notification.
b. Timestamp reconciliation and real-time-based dynamical support to continuously growing or decreasing sensor population within the network.
c. Real-time visualization in geographic context.

Wang et al. [29] highlighted three different schemes (i.e., wake-up radio [WUR], wireless energy harvesting [WEH] and error control coding [ECC]), which claim to improve the performance of green WSNs via reducing the CO_2 emissions. The multi-objective substructure resource allocation was proposed for green cooperative cognitive radio (CR) sensor networks [30]. Bedi et al. [31] proposed a hybrid transmission protocol that can maximize lifetime reliability guarantees for WSNs. The advantages of send-wait automatic repeat-request (SW-ARQ) protocol and network coding-based redundant transmission (NCRT) approach have been combined in order to improvise the results further. The SW-ARQ protocol has been adopted to save energy nearby the sink areas. A few of the highlighted aspects of green WSNs that can be dwelled upon for further improvisations are as follows:

a. Sensor nodes should selectively work when required otherwise in a sleep mode to save energy consumption.
b. Energy depletion mechanism should generate power from natural resources of the environment like the sun, vibrations, kinetic energy, temperature etc.
c. Optimization of radio techniques (e.g., transmission power control, cooperative communication, modulation optimization, energy-efficient CR and directional antennas).
d. Data reduction mechanisms and energy-efficient routing techniques.

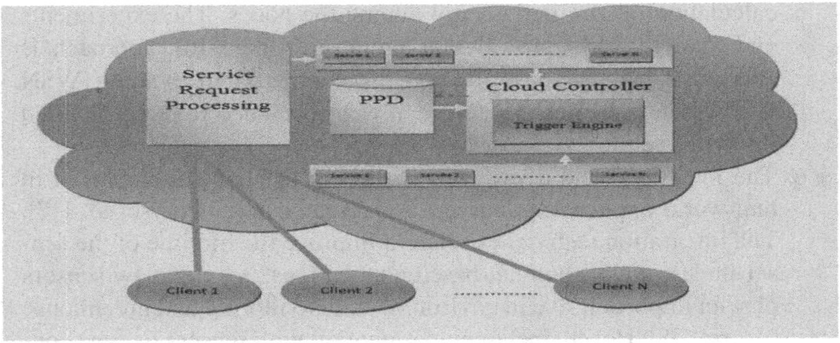

FIGURE 4.7   Green Cloud Computing Mobile Cloud Camera Laptop Desktop Monitor Tablet

4.9 GREEN CLOUD COMPUTING TECHNOLOGY

The concept of cloud computing (CC) is an emerging virtualization technology used all across the internet. It is currently capable of providing unlimited computational, storage and service delivery via the internet as conceptually shown in Figure 4.7. CC technology is ubiquitous in nature, whereas IoT is pervasive. The hybridized integration of both the concept, CC and IoT, together gives rise to broad future scope of research. The major focus of GCC is promoting the usage of eco-friendly products, which could be facilely recycled and reused. [32-37].

The recent GCC technology for the cloud is mainly designed to reduce the usage of hazardous materials, maximize energy consumption and enhance the recyclability of old products and waste. The green factor here can be achieved by product longevity resource allocation and paperless virtualization or proper power management. The concept was supported by a study, which covers the various technologies for GCC supported with reduced energy consumption [13]. Chen et al. [32] discussed in detail the use of integrating IoT in different applications such as architectures, protocols, service models, database technologies, sensors and algorithms.

The idea of GCC has been adopted by techniques designed mainly to minimize the power requirement. Asensio et al. [38] combinedly analysed the power performance of GCC and GDC. Though multiple efforts have been put to use to reduce energy consumption in public and private clouds during processes like switching, data processing, transmission and data storage [39], the reduction in overall energy consumed is quite insignificant. Some of the contributions carried out over GCC that claim to provide potential solutions are as follows:

a. Software and hardware techniques for decreasing energy consumption.
b. Power-saving methodology based on VM techniques (e.g., VM consolidation, VM migration, VM placement, VM allocation).
c. Various energy-efficient resource allocation mechanisms.
d. Efficient modes for energy-saving systems.
e. Green CC techniques based on cloud supporting technologies (e.g., communications, networks).

4.10 GREEN MACHINE-TO-MACHINE TECHNOLOGY

As discussed previously in the book, M2M is an advanced technological version of IoT, where machines interact with each other without human intervention. The commencement of IoT technology has made the billions of connected machines recognize, communicate and respond to each other. Various upcoming research and projects undertaken have been estimated to connect 100 billion devices over the internet [40-44].

Some related research works conducted over M2M include machine device access control (MDAC), which has been devised to achieve minimal energy consumption (EC) and also adapt to a variable distribution of MDAC [42]. Moreover, a cooperative technique has been proposed which could improve the power consumption of the cell-edge users and M2M-assisted networks. In addition to the highlighted techniques and proposed algorithms, Bartoli et al. [46], Datsika et al. [47] and Dayarathna et al. [48] discussed adopting necessary methods for designing and implementing a cooperating M2M communication network integrated with lower power consumption. Himsoon et al. [45], in their research contribution, discussed the framework that could exploit cooperative diversity in order to reduce the power consumption. There are various relay selection schemes involved in determining the optimal relay node, which ensures the decreases in summation of transmitted power.

The M2M nodes here communicate intelligently collecting the data and send it to base station (BS) for deployment within the M2M domain for wireless network relays. The BS also supports different M2M applications over the network in multiple application domains. The green M2M and the massive machines involved in M2M communications consume a lot of energy, typically in the M2M field. Some of the highlighted techniques proposed by researchers that can be adopted to improve energy efficiency for greening IoT are [7] as follows:

a. Intelligently adjusted power transmission.
b. Efficient communication protocols required for distributing the computing techniques.
c. Activity scheduling of nodes used to switch some nodes to sleeping mode while keeping the functionality of the original network.
d. Energy-saving mechanisms.
e. Employ energy harvesting and the benefits of CR.

4.11 GREEN DATA CENTRE TECHNOLOGY

Green data centre (GDC) is a new concept that aims at replacing the regular data centres responsible for data repository, i.e., data storage, data management and data dissemination. This data is typically created by users, systems, things etc. The data centres are responsible for handling various data and their related applications. The data centre (DC) here consumes huge amounts of power that has high operational costs and emits heavy CO_2 footprints. Numerous generations of big data seem to grow asymptotically due to the use of recent technologies like mobile devices, sensors etc. On the way towards smart world development, the energy efficiency of DC needs a lot of intervention in terms of effective power management as well as emissions of carbon footprints. Some researchers [48] discussed techniques that claim to decrease energy consumption. In support of the work contributed by authors [47, 48], others [49, 50] proposed an optimization method that improvises the energy efficiency of DC with supporting QoS. GDCs in the upcoming technologies have been employed to support data-related services for cloud-assisted mobile ad hoc networks (MANET) in 5G design [51].

The survey conducted by Mao [52] suggested few effective methods for reduction of energy consumption, keeping intact the cooling efficiency of DCs designed for greening IoT. Various energy-saving mechanisms designed for cloud data servers tend to decrease the routing and searching transactions adversely affecting the QoS. These challenges have been addressed by a few researchers. The article contributed by Peoples et al. [53] explored mechanisms that integrate effectiveness into an energy-efficient context-aware broker (e-CAB) framework in order to establish efficient next-generation DCs. However, another study [54] proposed a GDC concept with air conditioning supported by cloud techniques built with two subsystems: DC equipped with an air conditioning system and a cloud management platform. The DC with a supported air-conditioning system offers environmental monitoring, air conditioning, communication, temperature control and ventilation, whereas the cloud platform provides services such as data storage, big data analysis and prediction and up-layer applications.

Ant colony system (ACS)-based VM is a recently proposed hybrid technique used for reducing the power consumption of DCs while preserving QoS requirements [52, 53]. The ACS is a swarm optimization technique that is typically used to find an approximate optimal solution. Moreover, dynamic VM has been considered for reduction in energy consumption by cloud DC while maintaining the QoS [54]. Some techniques adopted to improve energy efficiency of GDC can be highlighted as [51, 52] follows:

a. Use renewable/green sources of energy.
b. Utilize efficient and dynamic power management techniques.
c. Design energy-efficient hardware.
d. Design novel energy-efficient data centre architectures to achieve power conservation.
e. Construct efficient and accurate data centre power models.
f. Draw support from communication and computing techniques.

4.12 GREEN COMMUNICATIONS AND NETWORKING

The role of green wireless communication is quite significant in Green IoT. The concept of integrating energy efficiency and power management within communication device nodes is currently the major focus for implementing the green factor within general communication and networking devices. The features of green communications and networking maintain within itself sustainable, energy-aware, energy-efficient and environmentally aware networking standards. The concept of green communication network refers to low CO_2 emissions, low exposure to radiations and energy efficiency. Many research works are conducted with multiple hybridized concepts such as genetic algorithm optimization for the network planning, which showed significant CO_2 reductions, cost optimization and low exposure to radiation [53]. A similar idea has been proposed in a study [49, 50], which discusses maximizing data rate, minimizing CO_2 emissions in cognitive WSNs etc. In addition, with the previous contribution of authors, Chan et al. [65] have come up with a set of models for performing the evaluation of the use-phase power consumption and CO_2 emissions in wireless telecommunication network services.

The analysis and exploration on the energy efficiency of 5G mobile communication networks can be described by three broad aspects: theory models, technology developments and applications. Abrol and Jha [66] have worked on the impact and the need for growth in technologies and the necessity of integrating energy efficiency components in next-generation networks (NGNs). The urge to adopt energy efficiency mechanisms and control CO_2 emissions is accountable to the fact of increased demands, enhanced data rate and high QoS of the NGN. Multiple research work by various researchers has proposed mechanisms to enforce energy savings by using solar and enhanced QoS. One of the highlighted concepts for the same proposal is applying network coding-based communication and reliable storage for saving energy in Green IoT [54]. The stochastic geometry approach for modelling traffic patterns is capable of concurrent execution efficiently to achieve a significant enhancement with respect to energy efficiency while maintaining QoS requirements [55]. A similar contribution of a utility-based adaptive duty cycle (UADC) algorithm has been proposed to reduce delays, increase energy efficiency while maintaining long lifetime [56]. The hypertext transfer protocol enhances the life span as well as reduces transmission delays improving the reliability aspect.

The 5G technology majorly focuses on reducing energy utilization, which may lead to green communication as well as healthy environment.

Currently 5G concept has incorporated features like enhanced reliability and QoS of the communication between machines. It also establishes large coverage connectivity, reduces latency factor, saves energy as well as supports higher data rate and system capacity. Some 5G applications and its services include e-health, robotics communication, interaction of human and robotics, media, transport and logistics, e-learning, e-governance, public safety, automotive and industrial systems etc.

4.13 GREEN INTERNET TECHNOLOGIES

The extensive usage of internet and communication technology in the next generation and much more has led to researchers working on the development of a smart and green grid [57]. The idea of a green grid majorly focuses on improving the power consumption efficiently.

A smart grid is an electrical grid capable of achieving a wide range of operations and energy optimization techniques, which includes:

1. Better facilitation of the connection and operation of generators having divergent sizes and technologies.
2. Allow consumers to play a part in optimizing the operation of the system.
3. Provide consumers with greater information and options for how they use their power supply.
4. Significantly reduce the environmental impact of the whole electricity supply system.
5. Maintain or even improve the existing high levels of system reliability, quality and security of supply.
6. Maintain and improve the existing services efficiently.

The technique of traffic and routers scheduling shows tremendous potential with respect to reducing the energy needs of the system as well as making its design and operations more simplified in nature [58]. One of the proposed mechanisms for the same is dynamic a topology management mechanism for the green internet (GIDTMM) [59]. Similarly, in the study [60], the concept of greening internet for wired access networks (WANs) in the data network has been elaborated where overall power consumption of wired access networks has been estimated [60]. Contradictory work contributed by Suh et al. [61] has explored the effect of construction equipment of data networks used for greening the internet. The green network design mainly considers factors such as estimation of power consumption and saving of potential energy consumed by data network equipment.

The study by Suh et al. [62] designed a green internet routing technique, due to which the routing can lead traffic in a way that is environmentally friendly. The idea is also highlighted by Yang et al. [63], which revealed the differentiated renewable and non-renewable energy for green internet routing. A similar contribution was provided by Hoque et al. [64], who examined technique solutions to enhance the energy efficiency of mobile hand-held devices for wireless multimedia streaming.

4.14 CONCLUSION

The chapter mainly discusses the various designs and strategies that can be adopted in order to implement the Green IoT concept into practice. It discusses in detail the energy optimization techniques and strategies including devices that can be used as a mode of saving energy. It highlights the various system models adopted to achieve energy efficiency in the Green IoT networks, followed by a detailed description of some energy-efficient devices that may be employed to achieve the expected level of optimization of power consumption. And finally, the techniques that can be adopted to convert an existing system into Green IoT with the help of smart grids, incorporating green elements within various networks. The chapter also highlights a few technical issues in areas where advanced technology has been implemented with green factors, which opens the door for further research.

REFERENCES

[1] A. Whitmore, A. Agarwal, L. Da Xu., "The Internet of Things—A Survey of Topics and Trends," *Information Systems Frontiers*, vol. 17, no. 2, pp. 261–274, 2015.

[2] T. Qiu, et al., "A Task-Efficient Sink Node Based on Embedded Multi-Core soC for Internet of Things," *Future Generation Computer Systems*, vol. 82, pp. 656–666, 2018.

[3] N. Kaur, S.K. Sood, "An Energy-Efficient Architecture for the Internet of Things (IoT)," *IEEE Systems Journal*, vol. 11, no. 2, pp. 796–805, 2017.

[4] A. Bagula, L. Castelli, M. Zennaro, "On the Design of Smart Parking Networks in the Smart Cities: An Optimal Sensor Placement Model," *Sensors*, vol. 15, no. 7, pp. 15443–15467, 2015.

[5] S.K. Datta., et al., "Web of Things for Connected Vehicles," *25th International World Wide Web Conference*, 2016. Montreal, Canada.

[6] P. Sethi, S.R. Sarangi, "Internet of Things: Architectures, Protocols, and Applications," *Journal of Electrical and Computer Engineering*, vol. 2017, 2017.

[7] K.K. Patil, S.M. Patel, "Internet of Things-IOT: Definition, Characteristics, Architecture, Enabling Technologies, Application & Future Challenges," *International Journal of Engineering Science and Computing*, vol. 6, no. 5, 2016.

[8] R. Arshad, et al., "Green IoT: An Investigation on Energy Saving Practices for 2020 and Beyond," *IEEE Access*, vol. 5, pp. 15667–15681, 2017.

[9] L. Atzori, A. Iera, G. Morabito, "The Internet of Things: A Survey," *Computer Networks*, vol. 54, no. 15, pp. 2787–2805, 2010.

[10] D. Jiang, et al., "Energy-Efficient Multi-Constraint Routing Algorithm with Load Balancing for Smart City Applications," *IEEE Internet of Things Journal*, vol.3, no. 6, pp. 1437–1447, 2016.

[11] Y. Wang, H. Qi., "Research of Intelligent Transportation System Based on the Internet of Things Frame," *Journal of Wireless Engineering and Technology*, vol. 3, no. 03, p. 160, 2012.

[12] A. Gaur, et al., "Smart City Architecture and Its Applications Based on IoT," *Procedia Computer Science*, vol. 52, pp. 1089–1094, 2015.

[13] S. Murugesan, "Harnessing Green IT: Principles and Practices," *IT Professional*, vol. 10, no. 1, pp.24–33, 2008.

[14] J. Gubbi, et al., "Internet of Things (IoT): A Vision, Architectural Elements, and Future Directions," *Future Generation Computer Systems*, vol. 29, no. 7, pp. 1645–1660, 2013.

[15] M. Vellanki, S.P.R. Kandukuri, A. Razaque, "Node Level Energy Efficiency Protocol for Internet of Things," *Journal of Theoretical and Computational Science*, vol. 3, 2016.

[16] M. Aazam, P.P. Hung, E.-N. Huh, "Smart Gateway based Communication for Cloud of Things," *Intelligent Sensors, Sensor Networks and Information Processing (ISSNIP), IEEE Ninth International Conference*, Singapore, 2014.

[17] S.M.A. Oteafy, F.M. Al-Turjman, H.S. Hassanein, "Pruned Adaptive Routing in the Heterogeneous Internet of Things," *IEEE Global Communications Conference (GLOBECOM)*, California, 2012.

[18] H. Jayakumar, et al., "Energy-Efficient System Design for IoT Devices," *Design Automation Conference (ASP-DAC), 21st Asia and South Pacific, IEEE*, Macao, China, 2016.

[19] Y. Amin, Q. Chen, H. Tenhunen, L. R. Zheng. Evolutionary Versatile Printable RFID Antennas for "Green" Electronics. vol. 26, no. 2–3, pp. 264–273. Apr 2012. https://doi.org/10.1163/156939312800030901

[20] S. Krco, B. Pokric, F. Carrez, "Designing IoT Architecture(s): A European Perspective," *IEEE World Forum on Internet of Things (WF-IoT)*, Seoul, Korea, pp. 79–84, March 2014.

[21] Qing, X., C. K. Goh, and Z. N. Chen, "Impedance characterization of RFID tag antennas and application in tag co-design," IEEE Trans. Microw. Theory Techn., Vol. 57, No. 5, 1268–1274, 2009.

[22] J.-S. Len, C.-F. Chen, K.-C. Hsu, "Improving Heterogeneous SOA-Based IoT Message Stability by Shortest Time Scheduling," *IEEE Transactions on Services Computing, vol. 99*, 17 May, 2013. https://ieeexplore.ieee.org/document/6517191

[23] Choi, J. S., Son, B. R., Kang, H. K., & Lee, D. H. (2012, November). Indoor localization of unmanned aerial vehicle based on passive UHF RFID systems. In *2012 9th international conference on ubiquitous robots and ambient intelligence (URAI)* (pp. 188-189). IEEE.

[24] Lakafosis, V., A. Rida, R. Vyas, Y. Li, S. Nikolaou, and M. M. Tentzeris, "Progress towards the first wireless sensor networks consisting of inkjet-printed, paper-based RFID-enabled sensor tags," Proc. IEEE, vol. 98, no. 9, 1601–1609, 2010.

[25] Nimrah Saeed., Maryam Murad., Mehmood Nawaz. "Survey on Single Path and Multipath Energy Efficient Routing Protocols for Wireless Sensor Networks". *Journal of Computer and Communications.* vol. 5, no. 5, pp. 1–11, January 2017. DOI:10.4236/jcc.2017.55001.

[26] Shalli Rani, Rajneesh Talwar, Jyoteesh Malhotra, Syed Hassan Ahmed, Mahasweta Sarkar, Houbing Song. "A Novel Scheme for an Energy Efficient Internet of Things Based on Wireless Sensor Networks". *Sensors (Basel).* 2015 Nov; 15(11): 28603–28626. Nov 2015. Doi: 10.3390/s151128603

[27] E. Yaacoub, A. Kadri, A. Abu-Dayya, Cooperative wireless sensor networks for green Internet of Things, Proceedings of the 8h

[28] K. Wang, et al., "Green Industrial Internet of Things Architecture: An Energy-Efficient Perspective," *IEEE Communications Magazine*, vol. 54, no. 12, pp. 48–54, 2016.

[29] Z. Wang, et al., "An Energy-Efficient Heterogeneous Dual-Core Processor for Internet of Things," *Circuits and Systems (ISCAS), IEEE International Symposium on*, Lisbon, Portugal, USA, 2015.

[30] S.F. Abedin, et al., "A System Model for Energy Efficient Green IoT Network," *Information Networking (ICOIN), 2015 International Conference, IEEE*, Cambodia, 2015.

[31] G. Bedi, G.K. Venayagamoorthy, R. Singh, "Internet of Things (IoT) Sensors for Smart Home Electric Energy Usage Management," *Information and Automation for Sustainability (ICIAfS) 2016 IEEE International Conference on*, Galle, Sri Lanka, pp. 1–6, 2016.

[32] Y.-K. Chen, "Challenges and Opportunities of Internet of Things," *Design Automation Conference (ASP-DAC), 2012 17th Asia and South Pacific*, Sydney, NSW, Australia, 2012.

[33] K. Georgiou, S. Xavier-de-Souza, K. Eder, "The IoT Energy Challenge: A Software Perspective," *IEEE Embedded Systems Letters*, vol. 10, no. 3, pp. 53–56, Sept. 2018.

[34] C. Zhu, et al., "Green Internet of Things for Smart World," *IEEE Access*, vol. 3, pp. 2151–2162, 2015.

[35] R. Coppola, M. Morisio, "Connected Car: Technologies, Issues, Future Trends," *ACM Computing Surveys (CSUR)*, vol. 49, no. 3, p. 46, 2016.

[36] W. Ejaz, et al., "Efficient Energy Management for the Internet of Things in Smart Cities," *IEEE Communications Magazine*, vol. 55, no. 1, pp. 84–91, 2017.

[37] S. Rani, et al., "A Novel Scheme for an Energy Efficient Internet of Things Based on Wireless Sensor Networks," *Sensors*, vol. 15, no. 11, pp. 28603–28626, 2015.

[38] Á. Asensio, et al., "Protocol and Architecture to Bring Things into Internet of Things," *International Journal of Distributed Sensor Networks*, vol. 10, no. 4, pp. 158–252, 2014.

[39] L. Da Xu, W. He, S. Li, "Internet of Things in Industries: A Survey," *IEEE Transactions on Industrial Informatics*, vol. 10, no. 4, pp. 2233–2243, 2014.

[40] S. Sivakumar, V. Anuratha, S. Gunasekaran, Survey on Integration of Cloud Computing and Internet of Things Using Application Perspective, *International Journal of Emerging Research in Management &Technology*, 6 (2017) 101–108.

[41] T. Le Guilly, P. Olsen, A.P. Raven, J.B. Rosenkilde, A. Skou, "HomePort: Middleware for Heterogeneous Home Automation Networks," *IEEE Pervasive Computing and Communications Workshops (PERCOM Workshops)*, IEEE, San Diego, CA, USA, pp. 627–633, March 2013. DOI: 10.1109/PerComW.2013.6529570.

[42] Z. Shelby, "Embedded Web Service," *IEEE Wireless Communications*, vol. 17, no. 6, pp. 52–57, December 2010.

[43] S. Albers, "Energy-Efficient Algorithms," *Communications of the ACM*, vol. 53, no. 5, May 2010.

[44] G.M. Lee, J.Y. Kim. "The Internet of Things: A Problem Statement," *Information and Communication Technology Convergence (ICTC), 2010 International Conference, IEEE*, Jeju, Korea (South), pp. 517–518, November 2010. DOI: 10.1109/ICTC.2010.5674788.

[45] T. Himsoon, W.P. Siriwongpairat, Z. Han, K.R. Liu, Lifetime maximization via cooperative nodes and relay deployment in wireless networks, IEEE *Journal on Selected Areas in Communications*, 25 (2007).

[46] A. Bartoli, M. Dohler, J. Hernández-Serrano, A. Kountouris, D. Barthel, Low-power low-rate goes long-range: The case for secure and cooperative machine-to-machine communications, *International Conference on Research in Networking*, Springer, 2011, pp. 219–230.

[47] E. Datsika, A. Antonopoulos, N. Zorba, C. Verikoukis, Green cooperative device–to–device communication: A social–aware perspective, *IEEE Access*, 4 (2016) 3697–3707.

[48] M. Dayarathna, Y. Wen, R. Fan, Data center energy consumption modeling: A survey, *IEEE Communications Surveys & Tutorials*, 18 (2016) 732–794.

[49] N. Cordeschi, M. Shojafar, D. Amendola, E. Baccarelli, Energyefficient adaptive networked datacenters for the QoS support of realtime applications, *The Journal of Supercomputing*, 71 (2015) 448–478.

[50] J. Shuja, K. Bilal, S.A. Madani, M. Othman, R. Ranjan, P. Balaji, S.U. Khan, Survey of techniques and architectures for designing energy-efficient data centers, *IEEE Systems Journal*, 10 (2016) 507–519.

[51] W. Feng, H. Alshaer, J.M. Elmirghani, Green information and communication technology: energy efficiency in a motorway model, *IET communications*, 4 (2010) 850–860.

[52] G. Mao, 5G green mobile communication networks, *China Communications*, 14 (2017) 183–184.

[53] C. Peoples, G. Parr, S. McClean, B. Scotney, P. Morrow, Performance evaluation of green data centre management supporting sustainable growth of the Internet of Things, *Simulation Modelling Practice and Theory*, 34 (2013) 221–242.

[54] G. Koutitas, Green network planning of single frequency networks, *IEEE Transactions on Broadcasting*, 56 (2010) 541–550.

[55] J. Li, Y. Liu, Z. Zhang, J. Ren, N. Zhao, Towards Green IoT Networking: Performance Optimization of Network Coding Based Communication and Reliable Storage, *IEEE Access*, (2017).

[56] L. Zhou, Z. Sheng, L. Wei, X. Hu, H. Zhao, J. Wei, V.C. Leung, Green cell planning and deployment for small cell networks in smart cities, *Ad Hoc Networks,* 43 (2016) 30–42.

[57] J. Wang, C. Hu, A. Liu, Comprehensive optimization of energy consumption and delay performance for green communication in Internet of Things, *Mobile Information Systems,* 2017 (2017).

[58] S. Keshav, C. Rosenberg, How internet concepts and technologies can help green and smarten the electrical grid, *ACM SIGCOMM Computer Communication Review,* 41 (2011) 109–114.

[59] M. Baldi, Y. Ofek, Time for a" greener" internet, Communications Workshops, 2009. ICC Workshops 2009. *IEEE International Conference on, IEEE,* 2009, pp. 1–6.

[60] J. Zhang, X. Wang, M. Huang, A Dynamic Topology Management Mechanism in Green Internet, Distributed Computing and Applications to Business, Engineering and Science (DCABES), 2014 13th International Symposium on, IEEE, 2014, pp. 203–207.

[61] Y. Suh, K. Kim, A. Kim, Y. Shin, A study on impact of wired access networks for green Internet, *Journal of Network and Computer Applications,* 57 (2015) 156–168.

[62] Y. Suh, J. Choi, C. Seo, Y. Shin, A study on energy savings potential of data network equipment for a green internet, Advanced Communication Technology (ICACT), 2014 16th International Conference on, IEEE, 2014, pp. 1146–1151.

[63] Y. Yang, D. Wang, M. Xu, S. Li, Hop-by-hop computing for green Internet routing, Network Protocols (ICNP), 2013 21st IEEE International Conference on, IEEE, 2013, pp. 1–10.

[64] M.A. Hoque, M. Siekkinen, J.K. Nurminen, Energy efficient multimedia streaming to mobile devices—a survey, IEEE Communications Surveys & Tutorials, 16 (2014) 579–597.

[65] C.A. Chan, A.F. Gygax, E. Wong, C.A. Leckie, A. Nirmalathas, D.C. Kilper, Methodologies for assessing the use-phase power consumption and greenhouse gas emissions of telecommunications network services, *Environmental science & technology,* 47 (2012) 485–492.

[66] A. Abrol, R.K. Jha, Power optimization in 5G networks: A step towards GrEEn communication, *IEEE Access,* 4 (2016) 1355–1374.

Impact and Application of Green Internet of Things in Various Fields

5

5.1 INTRODUCTION

As per the literature survey conducted, "Green Internet of Things (IoT)" may be defined as "the energy-efficient methodology typically designed based on hardware and/or software that is adopted by IoT as a support towards reduction of greenhouse effect via existing applications and services or reducing the overall impact of the greenhouse effect over IoT itself." As technology has grown, the advent of IoT has reduced the greenhouse effect [1–2]. With further improvisation and optimization, the industry claims to further reduce the currently generated carbon footprints with the implementation of various proposed strategies. The Green IoT lifecycle is purely focused on factors like green design, green production, green utilization and finally green disposal/recycling in order to ensure no or very negligible impact on the environment [3–4]. A number of analyses have been conducted by various organizations. Recently, a report published by Cisco Systems Inc. provided some major insights into the envisioned role played by modern IoT technologies. The report states various issues and challenges that can possibly be solved using the IoT making it practically irreplaceable. It specifically categorizes some of the world's most challenging development and sustainability issues, which is claimed to be solvable only via IoT technology specifying its worth in the current technological era [5]. One of such case studies have been conducted by the Food and Agriculture industry that statistically predicted that population of India can reach 9.8 billion around 2050 [6]. The prediction clearly indicates the need to increase food production all over the world at least by 70%, which necessitates the need to improve the farm productivity to feed the entire human race. Considering such futuristic challenges and thinking of possible solutions, the Green IoT concept is envisioned as a key technology that can play a leading role while implementing the concept of smart farming, also called precision agriculture.

Precision agriculture has been defined as a suite of IT-based tools that allow farmers to monitor soil and crop conditions as well as analyse treatment options using electronic devices connected via IoT [7–8]. The concept also highlights the importance of compatibility between aspects like implementation of the technology with respect to farmers' expertise.

Recently, Ijab et al. [9] designed an IoT-based platform, Smart Farm-Net, which can collect environmental data from various fields and store them on the cloud for further investigation and analysis [10].

Such highlighted cases have been identified in the book that makes it quite vivid that the concept of IoT is supposedly going to reign in Industry 4.0 and its future trend, thus leaving us only with the option of devising strategies, methodologies through which different issues and challenges related to both IoT and Green IoT should be solved, including its environmental aftereffects.

The chapter briefly discusses issues and challenges faced while implementing the concept of IoT and Green IoT in various industrial domains, the environmental impact of green devices, along with a similar used case, i.e., "Green IoT in Smartphones," which will include most handheld devices in future systems.

5.2 ENVIRONMENTAL IMPACT OF GREEN INTERNET OF THINGS DEVICES

As per the literature, the term "Green IoT" can be expressed as "the energy-efficient procedures implemented over an IoT in order to reduce the greenhouse effect of various operational IoTs [8]. IoT has been mainly used as a contribution towards reducing the greenhouse effect or optimization of

IoT through adding the green component that may reduce further the carbon footprint, making it all the more environment friendly [4, 6, 7].

As discussed in previous chapters, the Food and Agriculture Organization's prediction regarding 66% of the world's population will belong to urban areas by 2050 makes it clear that cities will have to raise their productivity regarding their way of operation and their resources. The major challenge here is keeping or providing basic resources, e.g., fresh water, clean energy, public transportation, safety and security, which need to be ensured with minimum economic, social and environmental sustainability. In this challenging scenario of multiple electronic devices being used in day-to-day lifestyle, the concept of Green IoT implementation works as the saviour of the environment. However, collecting, analysing and exploiting huge quantities of data generated by various heterogeneous sources that are spread throughout the city have other problems to address. Smart sensors have been used for pollution monitoring. However, their transmission power is limited for sending data in real time. Therefore, these sensors are attached to flying drones that make them capable of gathering data.

Apart from collecting data in real time, such drones equipped with gas sensors also focus on airflow behaviour capable of identifying the point source emissions, evaluating the concentration of CO, NO, CO_2 and NO_2 sensors for monitoring the pollution emissions in a particular area. The current major contribution of Green IoT in industry is mainly on maintaining a "pollution free environment and improving life quality within smart cities." Hence, the drone can be used as perfect device in many scenarios for monitoring and predicting air pollution.

Another such area where Green IoT has found its place is in waste management techniques, implemented within smart cities that are improving into smarter and greener techniques under constant improvisation. Various companies and governments are looking for a good means to maximize the collection level using artificial intelligence (AI)-based techniques and smart devices such as smart sensors, cloud platforms, IoT etc. Kasper et al. [18] and Fishbein [19] introduced an intelligent waste collection cyber-physical system for smart cities designed using an IoT-sensing prototype. The IoT-based sensing design prototype measures the waste level within the trash bins and sends the data into the cloud via the internet for processing and storage. Based on the accumulated data, the method of optimization manages the waste collection process via forwarding the workers' necessary action. The author proposed an improvised strategy for waste collection on real time, which indicates when trash bins are full. The workers are notified about the status of trash bags in real time, reducing the chances of waste overflow. The concept of IoT has enabled waste monitoring and management solutions for smart cities via integrated sensors in trash cans. Such proposed comprehensive systems support the cities evolving smarter, healthier and greener. The concept of an automated smart waste management (SWM) system employs different kinds of smart IoT-based devices like edge intelligence, cloud and smart IoT devices that support decision making and processing, which ensures employees following proper procedures while maintaining a clean and pollution-free environment, supporting the concept of recycling wherever possible [20]. The SVM is monitored in a real-time mode while communicating with the cloud storage system. The waste management technique designed is expected to foresee the hazard level as well as quantify the lessening of waste for sustainable development within smart cities.

5.3 INDUSTRIAL APPLICATIONS OF GREEN INTERNET OF THINGS

The Green IoT concept with features like energy efficiency and high adaptability with the environment has a wide range of applications as follows.

5.3.1 GIoT for Smart Cities

The concept of smart cities integrated with green component can be implemented for optimizing the urban flow management while ensuring the real-time response to problems. Recently, multiple criteria such as technological, economic and environmental evolutions like climatic change, economic restructuring, population aging and public finance pressures have attracted the attention of the scientific evolution into implementing the smart city. The GIoT concept can be found as applicable to smart parking; checking the strength of buildings, bridges and monuments; and traffic management on the street and intersections. In day-to-day life, GIoT can be used in controlling and monitoring smart traffic lights, smart bridges and vehicles to establish an economically smart city. The green factor is currently the fundamental requirement for various applications of this technology, which reduces overall electricity consumption as well as environmental damage.

5.3.2 GIoT for Smart Homes

The European Union (EU) Parliament laid the policy in 2002 that forced European countries into enforcing the energy optimization on the domestic front and in office buildings. Various research projects like SEEMPubS, DIMMER, AIM, IntUBE and DEHEMS deal with these problems. GIoT technology with the support of EU directives is used to manage smart systems with minimal energy waste within green smart homes.

Smart homes equipped with the GIoT concepts turn off lights automatically in case of residents leaving homes. GIoT-based air conditioners also auto-adjust indoor temperatures as per indoor activities with minimal energy. GIoT hence can reduce a building's energy consumption and associated costs by monitoring and controlling energy-related factors. Moreover, being green makes the living environment healthier.

5.3.3 GIoT for Smart Environments and Industrial Control

The GIoT-based advanced technology within a smart environment is equipped into detecting forest fires, analysing the air and sea water pollution, monitoring the quality of drinking water, controlling the surrounding areas and vehicle auto-diagnosis system and creating smart grid. Apart from mentioned application areas, the concept of GIoT can also be employed in various sensitive applications, e.g., liquid detection in data centres, quantifying corrosion and radiations at nuclear stations in order to generate leak warnings while monitoring sensitive data and buildings in order to prevent collapse. The criterion of being green ensures the shielding of the environment against any possible damage due to nature.

5.3.4 GIoT for Smart Agriculture and Animal Husbandry

GIoT technology has a huge application area with respect to domains like the agriculture and livestock industry to increase the quality and quantity of crops in order to meet future demands as discussed in previous sections. With context to the domain, GIoT can also be used in monitoring soil, moisture and pests of trees; establishing smart meteorological stations; and tracking as well as looking after the newborn baby animals. Adherence to green standards at all stages is necessary in order to produce healthy crops and healthy animal products for humans.

5.3.5 GIoT for e-Health

The universal focus of any technology including GIoT is into improving human health and well-being of mankind as the common goal. The GIoT concept can be used in monitoring medical refrigerators, well-being of athletes, patients' monitoring, measuring of ultra-violet radiations etc. In general, a GIoT-based e-health system is composed of tiny objects that can monitor body temperature and blood pressure (BP) and sensors equipped with limited battery power. Such applications switch the object into inactive mode when they are nonoperational in nature, i.e., power-saving mode in order to preserve energy. Moreover, CPU speed is reduced if there are no processing tasks. Considering the fact that such applications like GIoT are very close to humans, the green component is quite important as it is harmless to the environment. The reduction of the number of used sensors for monitoring the physiological signals is in line with GIoT goals. Hence, offering green brain-to-machine connections also plays a major role in brain-controlled GIoT applications.

The opportunities of smart cities' technologies incorporate within themselves many advantages due to the usage of IoT devices such as sensors, actuators, wearable devices etc. To improve smart cities, autonomous cars supported with many potential services and enabled by many vehicle-to-vehicle and vehicle-to-internet wireless communication may be considered as the technology disruption. It aims to changing the ways in which taxies are being executed and owned. For example, improving traffic flow and controlling accidents via intelligent systems and collaborative IoT devices are expected to improve the communication prospects within autonomous cars. The designed autonomous vehicles may onboard passengers over an on-demand basis including both onloading and unloading areas. The improvement of traffic flow may allow various public services into optimizing evacuation planning during natural disasters. As discussed earlier, machine learning techniques and IoT devices are necessary for improving efficiency. A smart waste management technique based on IoT uses data gathered regarding metrics like how much waste is produced as well as develops and implements models in order to reduce waste in the nearest future by processes of recycling and separation. The concept of IoT as of today has a major role in making our city cleaner, healthier and happier. It contributes to improving healthcare sector as well as the quality of life via monitoring and maintaining the natural resources gifted to the living creatures of environment and air quality and reducing health stress.

The industrial revolutions aim at improving and responding directly to the requirements and demands of industry in terms of productivity along with improving the standard of lifestyle followed within the society. Hence, it has been rightly quoted that "economic growth should always go hand in hand with each industrial revolution." Considering the continuous growth in requirement of power, the non-renewable nature of conventional sources and cost has inflated the price of fuel. This ceaseless growth in both price as well as demand has been identified as a barrier in industrial revolution for next generation. Information and communication technologies (ICTs) are the pillars on which tomorrow's innovative solutions are created. However, the smart embedded systems and the internet are two giant players carrying the ICT technologies forward. The overall impact of these can be seen in various sectors, including crossroads covering several industrial sectors: medical, manufacturing, automation, energy and others. The application areas of these technologies within the smart grid framework include integrated renewable energy sources used for optimization and efficiency.

5.4 CRITICAL PROBLEMS FACED WHILE IMPLEMENTING GREEN INTERNET OF THINGS IN VARIOUS FIELDS

A fewof the issues and challenges that open pathways for upcoming research pertaining to the areas of GIoT are discussed as follows.

5.4.1 Technical Challenges

Various technical barriers and issues that hinder the widespread implementation of GIoT are:

- Financial constraints and
- Hardware limitations.

These adversely impact the implementation of latest technology and concepts. Similarly, the lack of fast renewable materials or the incompatibility among various diverse materials put forth new challenges for GIoT. The GIoT should be capable of combining non-green networks with the green ones, leading to a heterogeneous structure. Some fundamental challenges faced while preserving green features in such assorted networks are maintaining green communication. Furthermore, a longevity of the participating devices is one of the permanent requirements in GIoT technology; hence, it is required that GIoT devices be compatible with a majority of application types so that post commercialization of the devices, their lifetime should satisfy customers. But the highlighting factor to be considered is that battery-based GIoT equipment should use green batteries.

5.4.2 Standardization

One of the major prerequisites of new technology is standardization considering its incurrent benefit add-on such as cost reduction, easy operability and quality maintenance. Deficiency of clear, defined and implementable standards for GIoT has led to the production of equipment and devices that are technically non-compatible with each other. Therefore, defining clear and robust standards is essential for GIoT expansion in the future. These standards have to be developed so they can cover the technical requirements of various applications. These requirements include the needs of industrial zones, factors integrated to ensure environmental safety and the needs of population residing in both urban and rural areas. GIoT standards are expected to be codified in order to optimize energy consumption as well as increase network resource capacity. The standardization also requires considering various available rules for the range of allowed frequency bands and energy levels for different radio communications. Besides these specified standards, various other standards also call attention green features of the equipment and objects. Considering the raise in the GIoT market and future forecasts, it is quite important to define standards for energy consumption, recycling, greenhouse gas (GHG) and harmful gas emissions to ensure that the human race remains protected from the effects of these harmful gases.

A few other related challenging issues that still need work are as follows:

- The re-design of Green IoT that needs to be tackled from the perspective of overall system energy consumption, subject to satisfying services' objectives and achieving acceptable performance.
- Designing realistic energy consumption models for various components of IoT systems.

Investigation on the following metrics:

    a. Energy-efficient system architecture.
    b. Energy-efficient service composition strategies.

   c. Situation and context awareness regarding users and applications.

   d. Energy-efficient cloud management.

5.5 CASE STUDY: IMPACT OF SMARTPHONES ON THE ENVIRONMENT IN PRESENT AND FUTURE TRENDS

As we know, the concept of green computing is highly correlated to the environmental sustainability, eco-friendly computing and IT infrastructure. It comprises all the physical ventures and efforts that are environmentally safe technologies and biodegradable devices within the entire life cycle of ICT. The green computing terminology is mainly denoted as per the methodology adopted as a practice and study of not just using the computers and servers but also disposing them, which includes hardware devices like printers, monitors and storage devices etc. in order to reduce its impact to minimal level. The various electronic waste causes emissions of gases, e.g., carbon dioxide, methane and other gases, which can be hazardous to both humans and other natural creatures in the ecosystem. These emitted gases tear down the green and habitability factors within the environment while causing damage to the global climate.

Energy efficiency is a vital factor for future ICT, considering the availability and increasing cost of energy. With the rise in the cost of power and the necessity of putting a check on GHG emissions, it is quite evident that demand of energy-efficient devices can lower the overall consumption of energy computation, and communications and storage will soar. As mentioned, reduction of carbon emissions as well as achieving energy efficiency is the primary concern. Multiple device manufacturing companies are constantly working towards achieving energy-efficient IT electronic devices, reducing the hazardous material usage as well as supporting the recycling capability of both the paper and the digital devices.

As quoted time and again, the "objective of green computing is about reducing the energy as well as analysing the after effects of ICT-based devices, mobile devices such as PDA (personal digital assistance), laptops and mobile phones or smartphones on environment", is mainly due to the fact, of increase in issues and problems related to the greenhouse effect, where the focus is that the environment should be less polluted, more friendly environment products should be invented and their promotion should be increased in order to provide

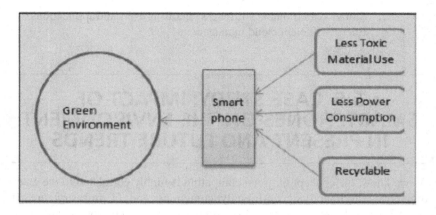

FIGURE 5.1   Green Smartphones

a clean and friendly environment. These factors have led to various firms and IT product development companies to move towards green computing, which includes smartphones as one of the main research concerns. Smartphones are found to cause harmful emissions to the environment. IT devices categorized as green should have three major focus areas, i.e., use of low toxic materials, minimal power consumption and use of recyclable materials [10-37] as discussed in Figure 5.1.

a. *Reduction in energy:* Various studies have been conducted to improve the power consumption and performance of the smartphones. Considering the fact that the majority of smartphones are created using metal, electric and electronic equipment has started concentrating on designing effective feature collections as well as recovery systems [11]. According to Zink et al. [12], sensitive analysis has provided an alternative option of replacing solar energy when electric chargers are connected. As generation proceeds, futuristic evolution of technological areas is expected to support more features and functionalities over low operational energy [13].

b. *Toxic material:* In the study conducted by Ning [16], the major highlighted issue responsible for environmental damage is electronic components. Smartphone chargers cause a lot of environmental damage as mentioned due to their main component, print wiring boards [15]. The amount of carbon footprints and CO_2 generated from the incineration of plastics was found to be almost the same as avoided by metals under use [17–18]. As stated, "Metals are harmful for the environment; the mobile phones are the more hazardous substances", where environment is concerned [19]. The Printed Circuit Board (PCB) from the mobile phone consists of 13% polymers, 63% metals and 24% ceramics [20–21]. The use of Cu (copper) in smartphones and the eco-toxicity within water seem to increase causing threat to marine life.

c. *Recycling:* The concept of separation of disposable material in order to overcome damaging the environment from various hazardous substances is called recycling. It is a process where non-degradable waste materials are converted into useful materials as a result of various processing techniques [22].

As per the survey conducted in the article [23], the majority of mobile phones produced in China are reused in the second-hand market causing low recycling collection rate. In a second-hand market, re-usage does not affect the environment in any manner. In the majority of the developed countries that are based on industrialization, approximately 15% of the mobile devices are returned for the recycling purpose in order to save the environment from further harm due to e-waste [26]. A few examples of mobile phone waste recycling activities are a green box environmental program and green card recycling activities [30].

A few reasons for frequent mobile phone replacements highlighted as per a study by Li et al. [31] are physical damage, software changes, incompatibility between the old version of hardware and latest versions of software launched in market, new additional features and apps being developed for smartphones to sustain in the market etc. As per the author in the article [32], the major cause of environmental damages is e-waste where Green IoT is achieved via managing e-waste that claims to reduce the hazardous substances to a huge extent.

d. *Green metrics:* The research conducted by Chowdhury et al. [14] suggests improvements in areas pertaining to energy efficiency of mobile system networks. Few special devices have been designed and extended currently in order to implement an eco-friendly environment that covers multiple energy-efficient metrics, collectively called green metrics. The various metrics considered can be categorized as [33]:

• The facility metrics
• The equipment-level metrics

The equipment metrics is accountable for less efficient rating provided to a single piece of the equipment of mobile network supporting specific functionalities within micro aspects. A few examples are the Telecommunications Equipment Energy Efficiency Rating (TEEER) by the Verizon NEBS Compliance [34], the Telecommunications Energy Efficiency Ratio (TEER) proposed by the Alliance for Telecommunications Industry Solutions (ATIS) [34], the Consumer Consumption Rating (CCR) [35], the Energy Consumption Rating (ECR) [33] etc.

The green rate here can be calculated on the basis of energy consumption of the network or power usage under any given scenario [35].

5.5.1 Reducing the Environmental Impact through Smartphones

In order to reduce the impact of smartphone emissions, a few highlighted points to be followed include choosing greener material, changing contract length, cutting down over-packaging and accessories and designing and implementing disassembly and energy saving batteries [36–37].

a. *Design for disassembly and repair:* The smartphones are designed to be glued shut or have permanent screws that stop customers from opening them. Designing smartphones in such low complicated manner makes it all the more to restore or exchange components. This process is more cost-effective and easily reusable where parts can be extracted and effectively reused in the second-hand market.

b. *Choosing green materials:* The use of polylactic acid (PLA) plastic made out of corn starch or glucose is both renewable and biodegradable. The choice of recycled plastic and ordinary substances for making smartphones is called for as an environmental-saving strategy.

c. *Energy-saving batteries:* The use of natural and organic radical batteries (ORBs) utilizes no heavy metals that may be dangerous to humans and charges battery in just 30 seconds.

d. *Cut down on packaging and accessories:* Almost 30 million new smartphones are offered annually where 70% of consumers are equipped with suitable chargers. HTC, Nokia and Sony are now promoting a few units with simple USB leads, needless chargers as a mode of strengthening the eco-ranking in the United Kingdom in 2010.

5.6 CONCLUSION

The chapter is a clear indication of how necessary it is to adopt the green factor in order to save the God-gifted natural resources that have both direct and indirect effects on the entire human race both currently and in the future. The chapter also highlights some of current revolutions major industries are undergoing while trying to strike a balance between innovative technology and the preservation of the environment as a whole opening the door for some major research to be carried out by aspiring researchers.

REFERENCES

[1] A. Sabbaghi, "Issues in Information Systems Green Information Technology and Sustainability: A Conceptual Taxonomy," *Journal of Internet Services and Applications,* vol. 13, no. 2, pp. 26–32, 2012.

[2] R.T. Watson, M.-C. Boudreau, A.J. Chen, "Information Systems and Environmentally Sustainable Development: Energy Informatics and New Directions for the IS Community 1," *Source MIS Q.*, vol. 34, no. 1, pp. 23–38, 2010.

[3] S. Brooks, X. Wang, S. Sarker, "Unpacking Green IS: A Review of the Existing Literature and Directions for the Future," in *Green Business Process Management*, Berlin, Heidelberg: Springer Berlin Heidelberg, 2012, pp. 15–37.

[4] "Greenhouse Effect," [Online]. http://news.bbc.co.uk/2/shared/spl/hi/sci_nat/04/climate_change/html/greenhouse.stm.

[5] C.C.D. US EPA, OAR, "Greenhouse Gases," [Online], 2015. http://www3.epa.gov/climatechange/kids/basics/today/greenhouse-gases.html.

[6] C.C.D. US EPA, "Carbon Dioxide Emissions."

[7] A. Khaldun, I. Arif, F. Abbas, "Design and Implementation a Smart Greenhouse," *International Journal of Computer Science and Mobile Computing*, vol. 48, no. 8, pp. 335–347, 2015.

[8] S. Murugesan, "Harnessing Green IT: Principles and Practices," *IT Professional*, vol. 10, no. 1, pp. 24–33, 2008.

[9] M.T. Ijab, A. Molla, A.E. Kassahun, S.Y. Teoh, "Association for Information Systems AIS Electronic Library (AISeL) Seeking the Green in Green IS: A Spirit, Practice and Impact Perspective," *IEEE 2017 International Conference on Communication Technologies (ComTech) –The green 2020: Impact of smartphones on the environment in present and future.* Rawalpindi, Pakistan, p. 1. DOI: 2017.4.19-2017.4.21.

[10] H. Falaki, D. Lymberopoulos, R. Mahajan, S. Kandula, D. Estrin, "A First Look at Traffic on Smartphones," *Proceedings of the 10th Annual Conference Internet Meas.- IMC'10*, New York, USA, p. 281, 2010.

[11] M. Oguchi, S. Murakami, H. Sakanakura, A. Kida, T. Kameya, "A Preliminary Categorization of End-of-Life Electrical and Electronic Equipment as Secondary Metal Resources," *Waste Management*, vol. 31, no. 9–10, pp. 2150–2160, 2011.

[12] T. Zink, F. Maker, R. Geyer, R. Amirtharajah, V. Akella, "Comparative Life Cycle Assessment of Smartphone Reuse: Repurposing vs. Refurbishment," *International Journal of Life Cycle Assessment*, vol. 19, no. 5, pp. 1099–1109, 2014.

[13] J.B. Legarth, I. Salter, O. Willum, "Repair or Buy a New One? The Environmental Consequences for Electronics," *IEEE International Symposium on Electronics and the Environment*. 2003, pp. 209–213, 2003.

[14] C.R. Chowdhury, A. Chatterjee, A. Sardar, S. Agarwal, A. Nath, "A Comprehensive Study on Cloud Green Computing: To Reduce Carbon Footprints Using Clouds," *International Journal of Advanced Computer Research*, vol. 3, no. 8, pp. 78–85, 2013.

[15] James Suckling, acquetta Lee, "Redefining scope: the true environmental impact of smartphones?" *International Journal of Life Cycle Assessment*, vol. 20, pp. 1181–1196, 2015.

[16] K. Ning, "Life Cycle Assessment of a Mobile Phone," 2005. https://eprints.usq.edu.au/499/1/KevinChinNingTAN-2005.pdf.

[17] K.I. Takahashi, M. Tsuda, J. Nakamura, K. Otabe, M. Tsuruoka, Y. Matsuno, Y. Adachi, "Elementary Analysis of Mobile Phones for Optimizing End-of-Life Scenarios," *2009 IEEE International Symposium on Sustainable Systems Technology ISSST'09 Coop. with 2009 IEEE International Symposium on Technology and Society ISTAS*, pp. 5–6, 2009.

[18] A.C. Kasper, G.B.T. Berselli, B.D. Freitas, J.A.S. Ten??rio, A.M. Bernardes, H.M. Veit, "Printed Wiring Boards for Mobile Phones: Characterization and Recycling of Copper," *Waste Management*, vol. 31, no. 12, pp. 2536–2545, 2011.

[19] B.K. Fishbein, *Waste in the Wireless World: The Challenge of Cell Phones*. New York, INFORM Inc., p. 81, 2002. ISBN: 0918780780.

[20] L.H. Yamane, V.T. de Moraes, D.C.R. Espinosa, J.A.S. Tenório, "Recycling of WEEE: Characterization of Spent Printed Circuit Boards from Mobile Phones and Computers," *Waste Management*, vol. 31, no. 12, pp. 2553–2558, 2011.

[21] S.R. Lim, J.M. Schoenung, "Toxicity Potentials from Waste Cellular Phones, and a Waste Management Policy Integrating Consumer, Corporate, and Government Responsibilities," *Waste Management*, vol. 30, no. 8–9, pp. 1653–1660, 2010.

[22] P. Rathore, S. Kota, A. Chakrabarti, "Sustainability through Remanufacturing in India: A Case Study on Mobile Handsets," *Journal of Cleaner Production*, vol. 19, no. 15, pp. 1709–1722, 2011.

[23] J. Yu, E. Williams, M. Ju, "Analysis of Material and Energy Consumption of Mobile Phones in China," *Energy Policy*, vol. 38, no. 8, pp. 4135–4141, 2010.

[24] G.T.R. Silveira, S.Y. Chang, "Cell Phone Recycling Experiences in the United States and Potential Recycling Options in Brazil," *Waste Management*, vol. 30, no. 11, pp. 2278–2291, 2010.

[25] N. Milovantseva, J.D. Saphores, "E-Waste Bans and U.S. Households' Preferences for Disposing of Their E-Waste," *Journal of Environmental Management*, vol. 124, pp. 8–16, 2013.

[26] P. Tanskanen, "Management and Recycling of Electronic Waste," *Acta Materialia*, vol. 61, no. 3, pp. 1001–1011, 2013.

[27] V. Thavalingam, G. Karunasena, "Mobile Phone Waste Management in Developing Countries: A Case of Sri Lanka," *Resources, Conservation & Recycling*, vol. 109, pp. 34–43, 2016.

[28] Y.C. Jang, M. Kim, "Management of Used & End-of-Life Mobile Phones in Korea: A Review," *Resources, Conservation & Recycling*, vol. 55, no. 1, pp. 11–19, 2010.

[29] E. Ponce-cueto, J.Á. González Manteca, R. Carrasco-Gallego, "Reverse Logistics Practices for Recovering Mobile Phones in Spain," *Supply Chain Forum*, vol. 12, no. 2, pp. 104–114, 2011.

[30] L. Zhou, Z. Xu, "Response to Waste Electrical and Electronic Equipments in China: Legislation, Recycling System, and Advanced Integrated Process," *Environmental Science & Technology*, vol. 46, no. 9, pp. 4713–4724, May 2012.

[31] B. Li, J. Yang, X. Song, B. Lu, "Survey on Disposal Behaviour and Awareness of Mobile Phones in Chinese University Students," *Procedia Environmental Sciences*, vol. 16, pp. 469–476, 2012.

[32] B.T. Tushi, D. Sedera, S. Dey, "An Archival Analysis of Green Information Technology: The Current State and Future Directions," 2015. https://core.ac.uk/download/pdf/33500865.pdf

[33] Rushan Arshad, Saman Zahoor, Munam Ali Shah, Abdul Wahid, Hongnian Yu. Green IoT: An Investigation on Energy Saving Practices for 2020 and Beyond. *Future Networks: Architectures, Protocols, and Applications,* vol. 5, p. 15667–15681, IEEE Access. July 2017 DOI: 10.1109/ACCESS.2017.2686092."

[34] Yuqi Fan, Hongli Ding, Lusheng Wang, Xiaojing Yuan, "Green latency-aware data placement in data centers", *Computer Networks: The International Journal of Computer and Telecommunications Networking,* vol. 10, pp. 46–57, December 2016. https://doi.org/10.1016/j.comnet.2016.09.015

[35] X. Wang, A.V. Vasilakos, M. Chen, Y. Liu, T.T. Kwon, "A Survey of Green Mobile Networks: Opportunities and Challenges," *Mobile Networks and Applications*, vol. 17, no. 1, pp. 4–20, 2012.

[36] A. Kipp, T. Jiang, M. Fugini, "Green Metrics for Energy-Aware IT Systems," *Proceedings of the International Conference Complex, Intelligent and Software Intensive Systems CISIS 2011*, Seoul, Korea, pp. 241–248, June 2011.

[37] J. Suckling, J.J. Lee, C. Energy, P. Advocacy, P. Report, C. Fy, Q. Song, J. Li, C. Lee, J.J. Lee, A. Zhou, N. Carolina, E. Report, J. Lane, IEA, "Low Medium High," *International Journal of Life Cycle Assessment*, vol. 3, no. 4, pp. 1–17, 2015.

Index

Note: Page numbers in *italics* refers to a figure on the corresponding page.

Printed in the United States
by Baker & Taylor Publisher Services